COME TO M

By the same author:

FAITH: THE GIFT OF GOD
A VISION FOR MISSIONS
THE MORAL BASIS OF FAITH

COME TO ME!

An Urgent Invitation to Turn to Christ

TOM WELLS

THE BANNER OF TRUTH TRUST

THE BANNER OF TRUTH TRUST
3 Murrayfield Road, Edinburgh, EH12 6EL
PO Box 621, Carlisle, Pennsylvania 17013, USA

★

First published 1986
ISBN 0 85151 471 5

★

Set in 10½/12pt Linotron Plantin
Typeset at The Spartan Press Ltd,
Lymington, Hants
and printed and bound in Great Britain by
Hazell Watson & Viney Limited,
Member of the BPCC Group,
Aylesbury, Bucks

★

Contents

PREFACE

The words 'I love you' are powerful words. And they are always fresh. Like God's mercies, they are new every morning. We do not tire of them. And yet – and yet that is not quite true. In one case we do weary of them quickly. That case is all too common. First they bore us and then we resent the words 'I love you' when we suspect their sincerity. And we suspect them when they are not joined with actions that suit them. We know how little it costs to say 'I love you.' We long to see some proof that it is so. Is it love indeed, or in words only? That is the question.

I will not say, 'I love you.' You might well reply, 'The writer does not know me. Why would he say that kind of thing? How could he possibly imagine that he loves *me*?' You might have many such thoughts. And, in thinking them, you might lay this book aside in disgust. So, I will not say, 'I love you.' But I do mean to say something similar. *To love someone is to seek to do him good*. And that is what I hope to do. I hope to do you good. Let me try to tell you why.

I am a Christian. Now there are some things that does *not* mean. It does not mean that I have lost all my selfishness. It does not mean that I love everyone as I ought. It does not mean that I am always compassionate toward others. In short, it does not mean that I am no longer a sinful human being. It does not mean that, and it could not. I am a man who struggles with my sin every day. I am a man who sometimes loses the struggle.

The fact that I am a Christian does mean one thing, however, that is relevant to this book. Someone has described Christian witness as 'one beggar telling another beggar where to find bread.' When one beggar does that for another beggar, he does him good. To that degree, at least, he loves him. Because I am a Christian I want to be like that first beggar.

My observation, for what it is worth, is this. Christians – and all, without exception, are imperfect – have this in common. They have heard the Psalmist's invitation, 'Taste and see that the Lord is good' (*Psalm 34:8*). They have come to Christ and found Him good beyond words. And they want to tell others about Him. They want to say on His behalf, 'Come to me, all you who are weary and burdened, and I will give you rest' (*Matthew 11:28*). And in that way they love the men and women around them. In that way they seek to do them good.

I do not know who put this book into your hand. Perhaps your bookseller. Perhaps a friend. But I am reasonably sure why he did so. He aimed to do you good. In that sense he loved you. And I join him in his aim. What I hope to tell you in these pages is the best thing I have ever found. I have nothing else to give that can compare with the knowledge of Christ. Hence, my invitation, my urgent invitation to you, is to turn to Him. To do so is, at the same time, your duty and your highest reward.

Come to me, all you who are weary and burdened, and I will give you rest. Take my yoke upon you and learn from me, for I am gentle and humble in heart, and you will find rest for your souls. For my yoke is easy and my burden is light.

(Matthew 11:28–30)

1: *Who Speaks?*

Let me give you the words of Jesus Christ again:

Come to me, all you who are weary and burdened, and I will give you rest (*Matthew 11:28*).

To begin with, one would not have to know anything of Jesus Christ to realise that these are gracious words. That lies on their face. But as soon as we ask how they might apply to us, things change. It is clear, for instance, that these are old words, spoken long ago. But I am a modern man. That poses a problem. Gracious or not, how could words spoken two thousand years ago bear on me?

That is not all. The words of Christ speak of coming to Him. Wouldn't that limit His words to His lifetime? He was a teacher in Israel when He spoke these words. People could see Him. They could touch Him. They could come to Him in the most literal sense. But all of that is over now. It ended at a cross. Or so it would seem. If these words were a proverb, some timeless truth, we could understand them. But it is not so. They are an invitation to meet a man who lived twenty centuries ago. How can this be?

The answer lies in the person of the one who speaks. Who is He? We know His name. We call Him 'Jesus' or 'Jesus Christ'. But that is not enough. Those names (in English, at least) do not help us. What is He like? What kind of man can issue such an invitation? That is what we need to know.

What kind of man is Jesus Christ? I can tell you in four words. He is the God-man. But then I must take the rest of this chapter to help you grasp what that means. When you see it, however, you will have your answer. You will know why He still says 'Come to Me'.

Jesus Christ is the God-man. He is both God and man. Let us first look at what we mean when we say He is 'God'. Right now that seems to be the hard part. Later, when we get hold of the fact that He is God, His being 'man' may seem difficult to grasp. But at this point that is not our problem.

I want to start by telling you what Christians do *not* mean when they say that Jesus Christ is God. They do not mean that He is like God in many ways. They are not using a figure of speech. Just now I am reminded that I have heard a handsome, muscular young man called 'a Greek god!' I think I know what was meant. This young man seemed to have reached the ideal of young manhood. He was *like* the fairest of the ancient Greek deities. In that sense he was described as a 'god'. But that is not the point in calling Jesus 'God'. Of course, Jesus was Godlike. I would not want to deny that. But He was Godlike for the same reason that I am Tom-Wells-like. I *am* Tom Wells, and He *is* God.

In saying 'Jesus Christ is God' I raise at least two difficulties. The first is this. It is hard to conceive how a man could also be God. Yet that is what Christianity says. That is what the Bible teaches. We are staggered by such words as these:

> In Christ all the fulness of the Deity lives in bodily form (*Colossians 2:9*).
>
> Christ . . . is God over all, for ever praised (*Romans 9:5*).
>
> The word was God . . . [and] the Word became flesh and lived for a while among us (*John 1:1,14*).

All of this seems too high for us. We hardly know what to say to it. For many, this is the 'offense' of Christianity. They will not have it that God has come in human form. That is the end of it!

In a way, I have nothing to say to such people. They need to sit submissively before the Word of God. If they will not do so, I cannot help them. But here I must be very careful. And so must you. The real difficulty may lie elsewhere. It may be my second difficulty. A man might say, 'I cannot see how God could come down to us in flesh,' when he means something quite different. He may mean that he could conceive such a thing *if, and only if*, he could think of some reason to require it. That reason would have to be enormous. And he knows of no such reason.

Well, there is such a reason. But it will make no sense at all until we find out who God is, this God who has come to us in Jesus Christ. So that is what we must take up first.

How does one describe God? There seem to be two ways. We may talk about what God is in Himself. We can use words like 'omniscient' (knowing all) and 'omnipresent' (present everywhere). There is nothing wrong with these words, nothing at all. Theologians use them all the time, and they are right to do so. But I do not think they will help us just now.

There is another way to talk about God. That is the way I hope to take. I want to describe God as He relates to us. By 'us' I mean 'ourselves as human beings'. That is a much more personal way to show who God is. It is like calling a man 'my uncle' or calling a woman 'my mother'. When we talk like that we show people in relation to others. That is more personal than saying 'He is a man and she is a woman'.

I have three names for God in mind. The first is *Creator*. The Bible teaches that God made us. We may say, 'God is *my* Creator. God is *your* Creator'. When we say that, we are not speaking impersonally. We are talking about how God touches our lives. We are His creatures. He is our Maker. That is how we relate to Him, and He to us. It is not necessary for us to know all about how God made us. That is beyond us. But the fact that God made us is of first importance.

When God made all things, He had some purpose in view. He made you and me with some goal in mind. If we were sticks and stones we could not ask what His purpose was. But He made us with intellect, with minds to grasp His purpose. We are able to ask the question, 'Why am I here?' We are meant to ask that question. And, sooner or later, we do ask it.

Here is one of the most striking facts about human nature. Men may claim that there is no God. They may say that life is without meaning. Yet they cannot avoid asking, 'Why am I here?' And they cannot escape the feelings that come in answering that question. Do not be surprised when men around you seem plunged in despair for no apparent reason. They have asked the question, 'Why am I here?' And they have answered it without God. Man may deny that he has a Creator. But he must live with the consequences of that denial. He must experience the frustrations and terrors of meaninglessness if he denies his Creator. God has made him that way.

But if God made us for a purpose, what is it? Why *are* we here?

Now I think you will see something important at once. It is this. The only one who can tell us why we are here is God Himself. We may be sure that when a person makes something he does it for some purpose. That is true of any person, whether God or man. A man, for instance, may make a kite. If we have not seen a kite before, we are sure to ask, 'What is that?' And we shall not be satisfied with the answer, 'It is a combination of sticks and paper'. No, that will not do. We will not let its maker alone until he tells us its purpose. 'Why?' expects an answer, and only its maker can give it.

In this way we come to see our need for some word from God. The Bible is that word. In it God has told us a great deal. And, especially, He has told us why He made us. Let us see what God has said.

Here, for a start, are words of Paul the apostle to a crowd of men at Athens.

> The God who made the world and everything in it is the Lord of heaven and earth and does not live in temples built by hands. And he is not served by human hands, as if he needed anything, because he himself gives all men life and breath and everything else. From one man he made every nation of men, that they should inhabit the whole earth; and he determined the times set for them and the exact places where they should live. *God did this so that men would seek him and perhaps reach out for him and find him, though he is not far from each one of us* (*Acts 17:24–27*).

In this place Paul tells us three things. First, we have a Creator. There is a God in heaven 'who made the world and everything in it'. Second, God has not abandoned His world. 'He gives all men life and breath and everything else'. Third, in words that I have italicised, Paul makes plain why God made us. '*God did this so that men would seek him and perhaps reach out for him and find him*.' You and I were created to know God.

But Paul said more to these Athenians:

> Therefore since we are God's offspring, we should not think that the divine being is like gold or silver or stone – an image made by man's design and skill. In the past God overlooked such ignorance, but now he commands all people everywhere to repent. For he has set a day when he will judge the world with justice by

the man he has appointed. He has given proof of this to all men by raising him from the dead (*Acts 17:29–31*).

Here Paul suggests the two other names for God that I promised you. If God is our Creator, He is also our *Lawgiver*. In Paul's words, God 'commands all people everywhere'. It is not hard to imagine God as Lawgiver. Since He made us He must know best how we ought to live. He alone could tell us what we ought to do and what we must not do. God's role as Lawgiver follows naturally from the fact that He is our Creator.

And then a third thing follows. God is our *Judge*. 'He has set a day when he will judge the world with justice.' Since God made us for His purposes He has told us how we must live. But He is not content to leave things there. At the end of history He will do something else. He will ask us what we have done with His laws. He will know whether we have aimed at His purpose. The three roles go together: Creator, Lawgiver and Judge.

Now let us look back a moment. In the past few pages I have tried to do two things. First I aimed briefly to describe God. After all, it makes no sense to talk of God coming among us if we have no idea who God is. But I also meant to do something else. I tried to lay the groundwork to answer the difficulty we looked at earlier. I am talking about the difficulty which says, 'I can't imagine a reason big enough for God to become man!' That is the hurdle we must get over.

The answer is bound up with what we have learned about God. First, God is our Creator. And He made us to know Him, to have fellowship with Him. Now here is the point. *If some insuperable barrier to knowing God developed, then we would have a reason great enough to lead God to become man.*

Again, God is our Lawgiver. And here is a further

consideration. *If some insuperable barrier to obeying God developed, then we would have a reason great enough to lead God to become man.*

Once more, God shall be our Judge. And here is the last point. *If some insuperable barrier to our passing His judgment developed, then we would have a reason great enough to lead God to become man.*

And that is what has happened. Each of these things is true. These 'insuperable barriers' exist. We could do literally nothing about them. They could not be overcome without God coming among us as a man. And so, that is precisely what He has done. In Jesus Christ we have one who is God in the flesh. He speaks to us with the authority that none but God has. We do well to listen to His gracious invitation, 'Come to me . . .'

2: *The Barriers*

In the last chapter I spoke of barriers that we cannot get over. These barriers keep us from knowing God. They hold us back from obeying God. And, eventually, if they are not removed, they will be our undoing in God's day of judgment. Now I want to show you how these barriers came about and to help you to see just what these barriers are. To do that I will need to take you back to the beginning of man's history.

When God finished His work of creation He 'saw all that he had made, and it was very good' (*Genesis 1:31*). That statement took in everything. It included man. At that point nothing stood in the way of man knowing God. God, of course, was good. Man was good too. It was natural that a good man and a good God should find fellowship together. And that is what happened.

The bond, however, between God and man was not yet permanently fixed. One fact stands out about these earliest days of man. They were days of testing. Man was on trial. And the trial was intended to show *how great a value man would put on continued fellowship and friendship with God*. The matter was not put just that way. But that was the heart of it.

What God did was this:

> The Lord God took the man and put him in the Garden of Eden to work it and take care of it. And the Lord God commanded the man, 'You are free to eat

from any tree in the garden; but you must not eat from the tree of the knowledge of good and evil, for when you eat of it you will surely die' (*Genesis 2:15–17*).

Here we see two things. We learn that God commanded man to obey Him, and we see that the penalty for disobedience was death. I want to look at both of these things more closely.

Does it strike you as odd that God's command had to do with eating fruit from a tree? That does not seem to involve any great moral issue, does it? At first sight, it seems almost trivial. I think that more than one person has stumbled over this. But there is no need to do so. The question, you see, was not whether Adam would live and die for some grand principle that both God and man must respect. That was not the question at all. The test was this: would Adam obey God?

You must have noticed how the human mind works. It likes to fool us. I remember reading of a man who was hired to plant cabbages. On his first day the farmer told him clearly how it was to be done. 'Take each cabbage plant,' the farmer said, 'and put it into the ground upside down.' The hired man could not mistake his directions. Now what would he do?

I do not remember how the hired man planted the cabbages, whether right side up or upside down. But I do remember the point of the story. At the end the farmer said, 'I was looking for a man who could take orders.' The farmer was not seeking a fellow who would agree with the way he wanted cabbages planted. He was looking for a man who would do what he was told.

It is easy to confuse these two things. We are likely to congratulate ourselves on our obedience when, in fact, we simply agree with what we are told to do. Is not that often the case? It may seem right to us, or it may seem wise. It may seem just the thing to be done, so we do it. But our doing it has little to do with obedience.

The best test of obedience to God is doing what He says simply because He says it. If it commends itself to our judgment, that is fine. But that is not the point. The point is this: will we obey, whether or not we grasp God's reasons? That would have been the proof of Adam's obedience. That is the proof of our own.

We do not know how long Adam lived before he broke God's command. It seems to have been a very short time, but that is not important. What is important is that Adam died, as God had promised. He did not die physically at once, though the seeds of death were sown in his body by his act of disobedience. His physical death was made certain by what he did, but the death Adam died that day was of another kind. Adam died *spiritually*. That is the heart of the matter. It is this 'spiritual' death that we must come to understand. It is this spiritual death that is the first barrier between us and God.

I told you earlier that Adam's trial introduced a question. That question was, *How great a value will man put on continued fellowship and friendship with God*? Now God had Adam's answer.

'It is all well and good to have God's fellowship,' Adam said in effect, 'but I must have my own way. That comes first. After that I will think about friendship with God!'

Now it may be that we have lived so long without reference to God that Adam's attitude does not shock us. We who live in democratic societies may come to think of God – if we think of Him at all – as a fellow citizen who must act by the rules of what we like to call 'fair play'. Let God map out His piece of territory and lay claim to it. What will it be? A square mile of choice farm land? The business district of a thriving metropolis? Or would God prefer the vast expanse of the starry heavens? Very well,

He shall have it! Only, whatever it is and wherever it is, let Him be content with it. We will respect God's rights to His own domain, and we will expect Him to respect ours!

The man who thinks in this way makes two errors. First, he misunderstands God. He has dismissed God from the roles God has chosen for Himself. To this man God is neither Creator, Lawgiver, nor Judge. But God refuses to be dismissed. We are fools if we suppose that God will be our fellow-democrat.

And there is one thing more. The man who thinks like this runs the risk of having God take him at his word. Does he want to be left alone? Would he rather that God did not interfere in his life? Well, it may be – for a time at least – that he shall have his way. But the experience will not be a happy one.

It is this desire for God to leave us alone that is meant by 'spiritual death'. Spiritual death is death toward God. A man may be quite alive to this world, and yet be dead. The smell of the grave is on the man who knows no longing after God. He may vibrate with enthusiasm at the prospect of money or power. That is common enough. We see it every day, and we speak of such men as vitally and wonderfully *alive*. But we are wrong. They are dead men, as dead as the fossil relics of some long-forgotten tribe.

Who, then, are the spiritually dead men of this world? They are the men who are content to be without God. *You* are a dead man if this is true of you.

But I must add a word of caution here. I have spoken of men 'who are content to be without God'. Let me tell you what that does *not* mean. It does not mean that such a man will find life satisfying. It does not mean that he will enjoy contentment. A man may be happy to be rid of all thought of God, but that will not make him a happy man. I must make this clear. I do not want to be misunderstood.

Let me address your own case. Perhaps you would not

call yourself a happy man or woman. 'See,' you may say, 'my very restlessness shows that I am not content to be without God.'

But wait! Do not be so sure! Your restlessness shows that you are not content. It tells us nothing about whether you want God to interfere in your affairs. That is a different matter entirely. Your dissatisfaction shows that you need God. Whether you desire Him is something else altogether. Let me say it again. To be spiritually dead means to be content to be without God. It does not mean simply to be content.

Now you may have noticed that in discussing Adam I moved from Adam to you rather easily. We were talking one moment about what Adam did long years ago. Then, in the next minute, I applied what happened to Adam to your own case as though no centuries had passed between. Let me explain why I did that.

When Adam and Eve sinned they were the human race. There were no other people on earth, just those two. In them, when they turned from God, the whole race turned from God. When they fell there were no godly people left. That much is plain. But there is something else to be remembered. If that were all, God might have waited for Adam and Eve to have children with whom He could have enjoyed fellowship. He might have forgotten the first pair and anticipated friendship with their sons and daughters. The wait would not have troubled God. Scripture makes clear that He is never in a hurry.

No, there was more, much more, to Adam's sin. In some way Adam stood or fell for all of us. That is why you may have heard Adam's sin called 'the fall of man' or simply 'the Fall'. When Adam and Eve brought forth children the children were fallen like Adam. They too cared nothing for fellowship with God. And their children, in turn, were like their ancestors. 'The Fall' is a fact of human life. It is as true today as it was when Adam sinned.

Early in the Bible we read this:

> When God created man, he made him in the likeness of God . . . When Adam had lived 130 years, he had a son in his own likeness, in his own image; and he named him Seth (*Genesis 5:1,3*).

The point of this passage is clear. Though God made Adam like Himself, Adam fell away from his first likeness to God. And when, in course of time, Adam and his wife produced children, they were like Adam. They were in Adam's likeness and image. They too were dead men, men who were spiritually dead and men who had the seeds of physical death planted in their frames, so that one day the grave would claim them. Eight times in Genesis 5 we meet some man descended from Adam, of whom it is said, '. . . and then he died.' After Adam no one asked whether this or that man would die. They only asked 'When?'

One barrier between God and man, then, is man's deadness toward God. We may also call it man's *corruption*. Man is corrupt at the core of his being. If that were not so, he would love and serve his Maker. But that is not his only problem. There is another barrier between man and God. That barrier is man's *guilt*. I want to take that up next.

You have noticed that people use the word 'guilt' in more than one way. Today there is a good deal of talk about psychology and many are interested in men's states of mind. Guilt is one of these. We say, 'George is full of guilt,' or 'Jenny is carrying a heavy load of guilt.' In each case we are speaking of a state of mind in George or in Jenny. Some men have accused George of not doing what he ought to have done. George suspects that they are right and now he feels guilty. Someone told Jenny that she should not have done the thing she did. Now a sense of guilt plagues her. Both George and Jenny are annoyed by these feelings, but the feelings will not go away. Later on I will have more to say about this state of mind. That is not the use of 'guilt', however, that we must grasp right now.

'Guilt' is also used to describe a man's standing before the law. This use of the word may have nothing to do with a man's state of mind. A man is said to be guilty when he has broken the law, whether he knows it or not. George may be guilty and Jenny may be guilty in this sense and have no inner conviction about it at all. The whole question may never cross their minds.

It is in this sense that guilt stands as a barrier between God and man. Man is a wrong-doer. Man is a sinner, a criminal in the sight of God. There can be no question of free and open fellowship between God and man as long as man remains guilty before the bar of God. The justice of God is at stake. Will He make laws and then allow man to trample them underfoot? That is the modern dream, but it is a lie.

> Surely the arm of the Lord is not too short to save, nor his ear too dull to hear. But [says the prophet] your iniquities have separated you from your God; your sins have hidden his face from you, so that he will not hear (*Isaiah 59:1,2*).

There the lie is exposed. As a lawbreaker man is exposed to the just penalty of his sin. He is guilty in that sense, whether he feels any 'guilt' in the other sense or not.

At this point I think someone is certain to say, 'But surely you can't be talking about me! I would never dream of trampling God's laws underfoot. Far from it! All my life I have tried to do the right thing. Don't I get any credit for that?'

Well, we will come to the subject of credit later. I quite agree that credit is precisely what we need. We need some merit, some credit, put into our account before God. But it is of no use talking about credit from our own good works. The Bible is plain: we have not done 'the right thing', you and I, and credit from what we have done is simply out of the question.

Nor can we say that we have *tried* to do the right thing. That little word 'tried' is likely to deceive us. When once we see how far we have come short we like to fall back on 'tried'. 'I tried,' we say, 'and I can't help it that I failed.' A man would have to be very unreasonable not to accept that explanation: 'I tried!'

But God will not accept 'I tried', not because God is unreasonable, but because the plea is not true. *We have not tried to serve God for His own sake.* To serve God for His own sake is the heart of all real service. In fact, we have done just the opposite. In serving God we have sought to serve ourselves. I know that because the Scripture tells me very clearly that all men are at enmity with God.

Here, for example, are words of the Apostle Paul:

> The mind of sinful man is death, but the mind controlled by the Spirit is life and peace, because the sinful mind is hostile to God. It does not submit to God's law, nor can it do so (*Romans 8:6,7*).

From what Paul says it is plain that man is in serious trouble. In speaking of 'sinful man' Paul does not mean to imply that some men are not born sinful. That would be the farthest thing from his mind. But Paul does recognise that some men have already been touched by the Spirit of God and to some degree have been changed. For Paul, 'sinful man' describes man in his natural state before God intervenes in his life.

Paul tells us, then, that sinful man's mind is 'hostile to God'. Jesus said the same thing in different words when He spoke of man's hatred towards Himself and His Father (*see John 15:18–25*). These are words that you may hesitate to believe, but they put one thing beyond doubt. They show plainly what kind of service a natural man will give to God. For, you see, *a man who hates God will never seek to serve God for God's own sake*.

Let me illustrate what I mean. Suppose you have an employer that you hate. We will call him Mr Brown. Will you serve Mr Brown? Yes, certainly. That is implied in the employer/employee relationship. You are hired to do some task and you do it. But could it be said that you serve Mr Brown *for his sake*? Not at all! If you loved him you might do so. But in your present state of hostility other motives keep you on the job. You need the money. The job offers prestige. You fear to be thought a failure. Or, your husband or wife would nag you unmercifully if you quit! Any or all of these reasons might keep you in the man's employ. They might lead you to do the best work possible. But the fact would remain: you could not be said to serve Mr Brown *for his sake*. That would be out of the question. Only if you dropped your hostility to Mr Brown could things change. Only then could you want to serve Mr Brown for his own sake. And only then would you 'try'.

And that is the way it is with God. So long as we are hostile to Him our service is marred. It is disfigured by the fact that it is not service to God for His own sake. It is always something less than that. The words 'I tried' are not true. They cannot be true, so long as we hate God!

Two barriers, then, stand between man and his God. They separate you from your Maker right now, if God has not intervened in your life. The first is *corruption*. At the core of your being there is hostility to Him. You are 'dead' toward God.

And the second follows from the first: your *guilt* before God. You have not served Him. With all your religion (or lack of it) you have done nothing out of love for God. Your most moral acts were spoiled by that one fact: they were never for the sake of God. You did not seek Him. You sought your own interest. In that you followed Adam. And Adam's son! And all of Adam's line – we are all alike – right down to the present hour. Any difference brought about in a man is purely and only a matter of the grace of God.

3: *The Meaning of the Invitation*

Let us look at the words of the Lord Jesus once more:

> *Come to me, all you who are weary and burdened, and I will give you rest* (*Matthew 11:28*).

There is the closest connection between these words and the barriers I have been speaking about, and I want to show you what it is.

Earlier I said that God became man to put aside the barriers that stand between Him and us. We have seen that those barriers are our *corruption* and our *guilt*. The problems are entirely on our side, in us and in our relation to God's law. That is why God became man. That is why we must listen when the God-man, Jesus Christ, speaks to us. We would be wise to pay attention even if His words were words of judgment and terror. But here we catch the sound of mercy. These are gracious words. He invites us to Himself. Let us see if we can grasp what that means.

At first glance the problem involved in coming to Christ seems to exist because He is not physically here. When daddy says 'Come here', or 'Come to me', a child knows what to do. He crosses the room, the field, the street, or whatever space there is between him and his father. In that way he obeys his daddy's command. For the most part it is not hard to answer this call when a small amount of space lies between two people. And if Jesus Christ were here we could answer His call in the same way.

But, of course, we cannot see Jesus Christ. And even if

we could, that would not meet our need. After all, the people who heard the Lord Jesus say these words were in His presence physically. Crowding closer to Him would not have given them rest. No, when Jesus said, 'Come to me', He had something else in mind. And we, who cannot see Him, may be thankful that He did!

The day Jesus spoke these words He gave the same invitation in two different ways. I think it will help us to put the two side by side:

Come to me, all you who are weary and burdened, and I will give you rest. (*11:28*)

Take my yoke upon you and learn from me, for I am gentle and humble in heart, and you will find rest for your souls. (*11:29*)

If we look closely we will see that each statement has three parts. The same brief outline will serve for each:

1. An Invitation (which is also a command)
2. A Description
3. A Promise

The first column has the invitation as we have been looking at it already. But note the second column. It too is an invitation, the same invitation. Both start with a command from Jesus. And both end with a promise. In each case it is the same promise, a promise of rest. Clearly Jesus is repeating Himself. He does it for emphasis. And He does it to make Himself clear. In this matter we dare not misunderstand Him.

Between His invitation and His promise Jesus has put two descriptions of men. In the first column He describes men who feel the crush of life. They are 'weary and burdened'. In the second column Jesus describes Himself. 'I am gentle and humble in heart', He says. Jesus is the very kind of person a weary, burdened man would like to meet.

I want us to look closer at the two ways Jesus puts His invitation. Do you see that Jesus evidently intends to make both opening statements mean the same thing? 'Come to me' and 'Take my yoke upon you and learn of me' are twins. What one means, the other means. *To come to Christ is to take up His yoke and to embrace His teaching*.

In using the word 'yoke' Jesus touched the world of His hearers in two ways. First, they came from a farming society. Yokes were a commonplace in their daily lives. They themselves plowed with oxen yoked together, or they often saw others do so. Beyond that fact, however, was another. The word 'yoke' had a further frequent use. It was used by the rabbis (Jewish teachers) of a man's obligations. They spoke, for instance, of 'the yoke of the Law'. A man in Israel was obliged to keep God's Law in its fulness. His obligation was his 'yoke'. If a man took up some new obligation, he took a new yoke upon himself. He was now bound in a new way.

A 'yoke', then, meant submission. When Jesus spoke of 'my yoke' He was calling His hearers to submit to His authority. His call was not first of all to a set of rules. He was urging men to be loyal to His person. Jesus was speaking as a King who wants His subjects to love and to trust Him as well as to keep His commands. And He does so still. When He says 'Come to me' He presses you to give yourself up to Him as Lord. You must never read His words as if they were impersonal. In the New Testament the Lord Jesus says 'Come to me' in many ways. Each time He is calling for your allegiance.

Sometimes Jesus urges men to come to Himself with the simple word 'believe'. It is a word that is easy to misunderstand, so I want to take it up next. But here, first, are some examples of Jesus' use of it:

> Then they asked [Jesus], 'What must we do to do the works God requires?' Jesus answered, 'The work of God is this: to believe in the one he has sent' (*John 6:28,29*).
>
> For my Father's will is that everyone who looks to the Son and believes in him shall have eternal life . . . (*John 6:40*).

Later on, the apostles put the same emphasis on believing in Christ. Paul, for instance, says to a jailer in Philippi,

> Believe in the Lord Jesus, and you will be saved – you and your household (*Acts 16:31*).

Clearly, to believe in Jesus Christ is the central part of the Christian message. But what does it mean?

To believe in Jesus Christ means to trust Him. If we think about what we do when we really trust any person at all, we will have a good idea of what Christ meant when He invited men to believe in Him. I want to pursue this for a moment so that the process will be clear in our minds.

Let me start with a distinction. In my book, *Faith: the Gift of God*, I put it this way:

> Suppose we hear a man say, 'I trust my wife'. Is it likely that he has just one event or occasion in mind when he says that? No, it is more likely that he means that he trusts her on all occasions. When we want to single out one act we usually say things differently. We say, 'I trust Michael *to* . . .' Then we fill out the sentence with the one act we have in mind. 'I trust Michael to put out the garbage.' 'I trust Michael to cook the pot roast.' 'I trust Michael to feed the cat.' If we say, 'I trust Michael,' without any addition, we often mean something more. That 'something more' is what we call *faith in a person*.

To make this clearer let me put it in story form. Suppose I am driving my auto from Cincinnati, where I live, to Chicago. That is a distance of about 300 miles, so I would be glad for some company. Along the way I see a poorly dressed hitchhiker. I stop and pick him up.

This fellow's face does not inspire confidence. His eyes have that beady look that is always associated with villains in western movies. In fact, it is not long before I wish I had heeded my wife's parting advice, 'Don't pick up hitch-hikers!'

Outside Indianapolis I see that I am low on gasoline. While I am stopped to get gas I turn to my newly found 'friend' and hand him a dollar bill.

'Here, take this and get us both a Coke.'

'Okay,' he grunts, and off he goes with my dollar. In a minute or two he is back with our drinks. But the errand has done nothing for his appearance; he looks as villainous as ever. In fact, I am glad to end the story here, just to get rid of him!

Now let me ask you a question. Would you say that I trusted that man? After all, I gave him my money. Isn't that trust? What about it?

The truth is this: I trusted him to buy us both a Coke. When he said, 'Okay', I believed him; I took him at his word. But you could never say, 'Tom trusted him', and stop there. You would come nearer the fact if you said just the opposite!

Let me quote my earlier book once more.

> The fact is, we often trust people to do this or that for us whom we do not trust in any extensive way. I may know that a certain businessman does not carry on his business in an honest manner. That does not keep me from trusting him to tell me what day of the week it is, or how far it is to the next town. But, still, I could not be said to have faith in his person. That requires something more.

What, then, is faith in a person? How does it differ from faith in a statement? Faith in a person turns out to be, not something different from faith in a statement, but the same thing on a much wider scale. *Faith in a person is a habitual reliance on what that person says*. Who are the persons in whom I have faith? They are the men and women whom I trust in their statements and claims generally.

Now this is what Jesus Christ presses upon you: *a settled attitude of reliance toward Him*. He asks you to rest upon all His claims and statements. And when you have done that you will have trusted in Him.

I think there is some confusion about this in the minds of many. It is so easy to say you trust Jesus Christ to do this or that for you. But that will not do. That is what is sometimes called 'easy believism'. It is Jesus Christ, the person, whom you must trust. You are not allowed to take up just one promise of Christ and rest on it. You must rely on *Him*.

I feel that I must pursue this further so that there can be no mistake about it. Many years ago I had a conversation with a girl I will call Millie. She was living an openly immoral life. The conversation went something like this:

'Millie,' I asked, 'are you a Christian?'

'I certainly am!'

'But, Millie, how can you live such an ungodly life and still make that claim?'

'I know the gospel as well as you do,' she countered. 'It says, "Believe in the Lord Jesus, and you will be saved." I believe in Jesus and therefore I am saved. Someday I'll go to heaven just like you!'

I am ashamed to say it, but back then I was at a loss to know how to answer Millie. I see now what Millie's problem was, but I could not see it then. It appears that Millie did truly believe that the Lord would take her to heaven. There was a good deal about the Lord that she did not believe in, however. She did not believe that He knew better than she did how her life should be lived. Of course she would not have said that. If I had asked her, 'Don't you think the Lord was wise in forbidding sexual looseness?', I do not doubt what her answer would have been. 'Yes', she would have said. After all it does not take any of us long to learn to say the right words. That is easy. But Millie's life showed that she thought she knew better than the Lord.

Now, of course, I am not Millie's judge. We may both be thankful for that! But the idea that Millie illustrates is very widespread. It comes to something like this: if I trust Jesus to keep me out of hell He will do so. Or this: if I believe that Jesus died for me I shall be all right. Or even this: since I prayed and asked Jesus into my heart, and I believe that He came in, I am now a Christian.

What do these ideas have in common? Each of them *may* – I emphasise the *may* – each of them *may* fall far short of faith in Christ in any comprehensive sense. They *may* represent something much less than faith in Jesus Christ as a person.

Follow me closely here; I do not wish to be misunderstood. No one knows better than I that a new Christian may not be able to set forth his faith in a way that would satisfy a theologian. For that reason a true Christian might *say* any of the things I have mentioned above. He might truly trust Christ and describe his faith by the simple words, 'I believe Christ died for me', or 'I believe Jesus will keep me out of hell'. I would not want to deny that. A man or woman can be a Christian in the fullest sense without being skilled at analysing all that is going on in his or her heart. Or without being good at expressing it!

But here is the point. In our anxiety that you should become a Christian we may offer you something less than Jesus Christ Himself. We may isolate one promise and offer you that. Yet that will not do. It is not enough. It is not this or that promise you are to trust, but a person. And when you believe in Jesus Christ you will not find it hard to believe that His commands are as important as His promises. You will think that each was shaped by the same immeasurable wisdom. And in thinking that, you will be right!

If you have followed me thus far, you will see, I think, why the Lord Jesus spoke as He did. 'Come to me' is a good way to express what He asks of you. So also is 'Take my yoke upon you and learn from me'. At first glance these may seem to be different things. But each says 'Trust *Me,* believe in *Me*, follow *Me*'. That is what 'coming to Jesus' is all about.

There is one more word that describes the change that Jesus is pressing upon you. That word is 'repent'. I want to take it up next.

In simplest terms, 'to repent' means 'to change one's mind'. The word, by itself, does not tell you what you are to change your mind about. You need the whole Scripture to tell you that. But there is the root of the matter. When you are told to 'repent' you are commanded to change your mind.

Some Christians object to the phrase, 'change your mind'. They do not like it, I think, because we so often 'change our minds' about trivial things. A man may want an ice-cream cone. He settles on strawberry. Then, just before it is dipped up, he picks another flavor. 'I think I'll have chocolate instead; I've changed my mind!' How easy it is, in this instance, to change one's mind! It makes not one particle's worth of difference in this ice-cream lover's way of life.

The Bible's command to repent is of another kind. It calls for a comprehensive change of mind. No cranny of a man's being is left undisturbed when he repents in the biblical sense. He has new values. He sees life differently. New feelings excite him. And I must not leave out his actions: they are turned about, in the direction of godliness. When a man 'changes his mind' in this sense, his 'mind' is equivalent to his entire inner life.

How would you change if you were to repent? Well, for one thing, you would have a change of mind about God. Let me tell you the extremes a man's mind is likely to run to when he thinks of God. You will know better than I whether what I say describes yourself.

On the one hand a man will often put thoughts of God as far from himself as possible. That extreme is to avoid God. Paul spoke of men who 'did not think it worthwhile to retain the knowledge of God' (*Romans 1:28*). To a natural man it often seems desirable to ignore his Creator. It has to be done, he fancies, in order to get on with the 'important things' (such things as pursuing his own career and ambitions). God, he is sure, will not be offended. For, of course, no offense is intended!

> In his pride the wicked does not seek him; in all his thoughts there is no room for God (*Psalm 10:4*).

How easy it is for a man to cast off all serious thoughts of God!

But there is another extreme. A man may often think of God . . . as a means to his own ends! He is poor, and God is a means to prosperity. He is sick, and God is the way to health. He is in danger, but courting God may yet bring him safety. How convenient, in these cases, to fall back on God! No wonder Paul warned against men 'who think godliness is a means to financial gain' (*I Timothy 6:5*)!

And how will you think of God, if you repent? How will your mind be changed? In this way: you will begin to be attracted to the God of Scripture. God will seem worthy to be known for who He is. You will realise the folly of thinking of God as the means to some 'higher' end. You will not only pray the prayer, 'Thy will be done' (as you may have prayed it many times before), but you will rejoice in praying it, even in adversity and pain. I do not say that you will never again give in to the extremes I have mentioned above. You will not be perfect, nor on the verge of perfection! But you will look on avoiding the thought of God, or using Him for your own ends, as temptations against which you must fight. And you will frequently win the fight!

You will also have a change of mind about the barriers I have spoken of. Take the matter of *guilt*. It may be that right now your guilt troubles you for two reasons. First, it makes you uncomfortable, and second, it may send you to hell. But, if you repent, a third thing will come into play. It is this. You will hate the thought of grieving your Maker. It will seem to you the height of ingratitude and thanklessness to offend the gracious God.

And as for your *corruption*, you will view it in a new light. In fact, it may not be too much to say that you will glimpse the depth of it for the first time. But that is not a bad thing. Quite the opposite! It is a giant step in coming to appreciate our Savior, the Lord Jesus. You will set a new value on Christ when you see the pit from which He will save you.

So there you have it, the meaning of Jesus' invitation, 'Come to me . . .' It means to believe in Him, to trust Him, and to learn from Him. It means to take a new view of God and of your guilt and corruption. It means a thorough change of mind. It means submission to Another and seeking to do His will. In a word, it means taking up a new life and leaving the old life behind. All of that is implied in coming to Christ.

In the following chapters you will hear the Lord Jesus say repeatedly, 'Come to me!' I hope you will listen.

But suppose you had a friend you wanted *me* to believe in, and to whom I should entrust *my life*. How would you go about convincing me? Would you say, 'Believe, believe, believe!'? I do not think so. That would not be the wisest way. And it is not what I hope to do in the rest of this book.

No, if you had a friend whom you wanted me to trust, *you would show me your friend*! It would be necessary, of course, to tell me to trust him. You might do that more than once. But that would not be the main burden of your conversation. Instead you would tell me of his qualities and show me his character. That is what you would do if you were wise. And that is what I want to do in your case.

In the following chapters I hope you will hear Jesus saying 'Come to me' and 'Believe in me'. And I pray that you will respond. But I have the most pleasant part of my task in front of me. I want to tell you in detail about the Lord Jesus. I will seek to display Him in His person and work. No Christian could ask for a more satisfying task. I trust you will join me.

4: *Come to Me . . . as Savior*

I am pretty sure that when most of us who live in the western world hear the word 'savior' it brings Jesus Christ to mind. We think of 'Savior' with a capital 'S'. In a way, it is quite right that we do so. 'Savior' has become a proper name, a synonym for Jesus. But, of course, 'savior' need not have a capital 's' and it need not be a proper name at all. In fact, in making it a proper name we run the risk of losing its original meaning. A man may think of Jesus when he hears 'Savior', without calling up any part of the meaning that the word conveyed when it first was applied to Him.

A savior, obviously, is a deliverer. He is a rescuer, a liberator. Implied in the word is the notion that the man to be delivered is in some danger, a danger from which he is not able to save himself. Then his rescuer steps in, either to destroy the thing that threatens him, or to take him where he is beyond its reach. Afterwards we may speak of the man as having been 'saved', and his rescuer as his 'savior'. There are fictional saviors, white knights who care nothing for the flaming nostrils of assorted dragons, if only they may rescue damsels from being fatally scorched. There are real-life saviors also, the heroes of a mine disaster, or the troops who stem the tide of a foreign invasion at the cost of their own lives. A country or a nation may owe its future to the zeal of such men. 'Savior' is not too high a title for each and all of them.

Let us see now how all this applies to the Lord Jesus. Why do we call Him 'Savior'?

There is first the matter of danger. If we ask what danger mankind is in, we have already seen something of the answer. Man is guilty and corrupt. These barriers keep him from knowing and obeying God. And, eventually, they will be his downfall when he stands before God as Judge. That is man's danger. For as surely as God is Creator and Lawgiver, He is Judge as well. There can be no doubt about that. We might have drawn that conclusion without our Bibles. God made man for God's own purposes. He told us to live so as to aim at His goals. It can be no surprise, then, if He calls us to account for what we have done, or not done. We can expect nothing less than that.

But, of course, that will be our undoing. We must ask what the Psalmist asked more than two thousand years ago:

> If you, O Lord, kept a record of sins . . . who could stand? (*Psalm 130:3*).

The answer is obvious: none could stand. No one at all! Our danger, however, is not the whole story. If that were not so, there would be no point to this book.

Over against our danger stands the Lord Jesus. In Jesus Christ the word 'Savior' comes into its own. In fact, in translating from Greek into English, if we want to catch the meaning of the name 'Jesus' in one word, 'Savior' is the word we must use. Just before Jesus' birth Joseph was told what He should be named:

> You are to give him the name Jesus [the angel said], because he will save his people from their sins (*Matthew 1:21*).

That verse neatly sums it up. The Savior is Jesus; our danger comes from the guilt and corruption of our sins.

I want to come first to this matter of guilt. When you hear Jesus say 'Come to me' in this chapter, I want you to understand Him to mean 'Come to me for forgiveness'. To be saved from sin is more than having your guilt taken away. Much more! But that is the place for you to start. It is of the sinner's guilt, taken away by forgiveness, that Jesus first speaks when He says, 'Come to me . . . as Savior'.

If I were to say that it was quite hard for God to forgive you, what would you think? I believe I know what would happen. You would misunderstand me, and it would not be your fault. My words might seem to imply a reluctance on God's part, as though I meant that God could hardly bring Himself to pardon you, or that His forgiveness – if and when it might come – would be half-hearted or grudging. But I would not mean that. Not at all!

I want, however, to hold fast to my words. They are the key to the greatness of Christ as Savior. God does not save sinners reluctantly, but He does so at great cost. It is not hard for God to bring Himself to rescue men, but the way He chose to do it brought enormous pain and sorrow on Christ. Christ suffered the full penalty connected with the breaking of God's law. That is the sense in which it was 'hard'.

The scandal of Christianity is the God-man dying on a cross. Jesus was not born in regal splendor. Nor did He pass His life in ease. Far from it! But what is all of that compared to the way His life on earth ended? There He is, mocked and despised by men for whom He prays; and there, at the cross, He is apparently forgotten by the One He had called 'Father'. Yet this terrific sight reveals the heart of our message. If you want forgiveness you will find it in His death. You will find it here or not at all. It is His death that brings the penitent sinner pardon.

Just now, as I finished the last paragraph, I experienced

a bit of a misgiving. My fear is this. Even though I have told you that the cross is of first importance I can imagine someone saying, 'Yes, yes, of course! We've always heard that; we know that. Now let's get on with it!' But there is no 'getting on with' Christianity unless you linger here. I hope to make that plainer in what follows.

Here are Jesus' own words, summing up the meaning of His life. Calling Himself 'the Son of Man', He says,

> For even the Son of Man did not come to be served, but to serve, and *to give his life a ransom for many* (*Mark 10:45*).

Then, after the death of Jesus, His apostle Paul says,

> Jews demand miraculous signs and Greeks look for wisdom, but *we preach Christ crucified*: a stumbling-block to Jews and foolishness to Gentiles . . . (*I Corinthians 1:22,23*).

Again Paul writes,

> For I resolved to know nothing while I was with you except *Jesus Christ and him crucified* (*I Corinthians 2:2*).

Once more he says,

> But God forbid that I should glory, *save in the cross of our Lord Jesus Christ*, by whom the world is crucified unto me, and I unto the world (*Galatians 6:14 KJV*).

Each of these quotations is a fair sample of the New Testament view. The death of Christ is the center from which all else takes its meaning. Why did Christ come? *Christ came to die*.

The death of Christ raises two questions. The first is this. How could you or I possibly benefit from the death of Jesus Christ? What connection can there be between His death and the forgiveness of our sins? That is the first question. The second has to do with His motives. Why would Christ want to come to earth to suffer pain and rejection? What moved Him? To find answers to these questions, it will be well to start with the words of Jesus quoted above, in which He says that He came 'to give his life a *ransom* for many'. In calling His life 'a ransom' Jesus gives us a key to the link between His death and the forgiveness of sins.

Nowadays, I think, we most often hear the word 'ransom' applied to a kidnapping case. Some prominent person (or the child of such a person) disappears. Then a relative finds a note or receives a phone call which tells the story.

'If you ever want to see James Brown alive again you had better see to it that we get one million dollars before daybreak. If you co-operate he will be returned unharmed. I don't need to tell you what will happen if you don't!' An exchange is demanded: dollars for Brown!

A ransom, then, is an exchange. Most often the exchange involves money, but that is not necessary. It might be anything. If they wanted to, the kidnappers could demand another person as ransom: Smith for Brown, or else! In that case one life would be given for the other. There would be a *substitution*. Mr Smith would take Mr Brown's place.

It is this idea of the substitution of one life for another that the Lord Jesus has in mind when He speaks of His own life as 'a ransom for many'. What He suffers, the 'many' ought to have suffered. His death is a death in their place. In dying He honors the law they defied. The punishment that they deserved falls on Him instead. His pain is the result of their guilt.

Long before Jesus was born the prophet Isaiah described this exchange:

> Surely he took up our infirmities and carried our sorrows, yet we considered him stricken by God,

> smitten by him, and afflicted. But he was pierced for our transgressions, he was crushed for our iniquities; the punishment that brought us peace was upon him, and by his wounds we are healed. We all, like sheep, have gone astray, each of us has turned to his own way; and the LORD has laid on him the iniquity of us all . . . It was the LORD's will to crush him . . . the Lord makes his life a guilt offering (*Isaiah 53:4–6, 10*).

These awful words deserve our closest attention.

When a man comes to sense even a little of his own guilt he is likely to cast about for relief. If guilt, to him, means simply the dreary feeling that distracts him from the business he has in hand he will seek to escape that distraction, perhaps by plunging more deeply into his work. He may succeed or he may fail. From the feeling of guilt it is notoriously difficult to escape.

But what can a man do who sees his guilt as the Lord sees it? What hope is there for the one who has been legally judged an offender before the bar of the Almighty? Where shall a man flee who has broken the Law of God? This is a fearful question because it involves more than the man and his feelings. It touches upon every aspect of God's character. Is God just? Yes, of course. Will He change? No, He will not.

'Where shall I run, then?' asks the sinner. 'Where shall I go to get out of His grip? I cannot survive the judgment of a holy God!' Well now, here is the good news. If you are *that* man, the sinner in the way to despair, Isaiah is the prophet for you! He is the prophet of *substitution*, the prophet of mercy worked out by a just and righteous God!

Look again at Isaiah's words. I mean such words concerning Jesus as these:

> Surely he took up *our* infirmities . . .
> [He] carried *our* sorrows . . . (*v.4*)
> He was pierced for *our* transgressions . . .

He was crushed for *our* iniquities . . . (*v.5*)
And the LORD has laid on him the iniquity *of us all* . . . (*v.6*)

Here we have God's way of forgiveness. The Lord has crushed the God-man in our stead, says Isaiah. 'He swapped with me!' said a Welsh miner. Yes, He did – and He will 'swap' with you, too, if you come to Him. Christ will trade His righteousness for your sin. That is what He will do if you turn to Him just now.

But perhaps you will want to ask a question that is likely to come into the mind of anyone who takes this way of salvation seriously: How can it be right and fair for God to punish the Lord Jesus in my place, so that I may go free? I am the law breaker. Can that be just? Is not that more than a little like giving my neighbor a beating when I misbehave? Where is the justice in that?

Now in one sense this question is unnecessary. We may say, and say it with certainty, that if God has set out to save sinners in this way, then, without a doubt, it is right and fair. We may say this, and we must! This too is involved in trusting in God, in believing in Christ. It is useless to say that we are penitent if we are still ready to sit in judgment over the works of Almighty God when we do not understand them. That would be a strange repentance indeed!

The Bible does, however, throw light on this question in the following way. It tells me that I must never think of the Lord Jesus as an unwilling victim. It is not a case of God getting hold of Jesus and giving Him what I deserved whether He wanted it or not. Just the opposite! As God the Son, He is a chief party to the plan. Here is how the Lord Jesus Himself saw His own death:

I lay down my life for the sheep . . . only to take it up again. No-one takes it from me, but I lay it down of my own accord. I have authority to lay it down and authority to take it up again. This command I received from my Father (*John 10:15, 17, 18*).

These words do not mean that Jesus felt no difficulty in dying, but they show that He did not go reluctantly to the cross. To go or not to go was wholly within His power. It was in no sense thrust upon Him. In fact, we may go a step further and say that it was His very determination to do the will of God in dying for His sheep that overcame the pain and agony and horror and shame of crucifixion.

In closing this chapter I want to come to the second point I made about the death of Christ, the question of His motives. What moved Christ to suffer pain and scorn and rejection? Suppose we grant that He came into the world to die, what moved Him?

There are really two answers to this question, but they can be summed up under a single word: love. It is important to grasp why I have said 'two answers' rather than one. If we hear that Jesus died for love's sake we will quite naturally think that it is love for ourselves that is meant. And so it is, in part. I will come to that in a moment. But that is not the first thing. There is another love here: Christ's love for His Father in heaven and for the character of His Father.

Let me ask you a question. If Jesus could have bought forgiveness for you and for me without regard to God's glory, would He have done it? Suppose there had been some short cut to our salvation in which He might have ignored God's justice, would Jesus have taken it? Ask yourself this: if Jesus Christ could have brought us happiness for ever without thinking of the rightness or wrongness of His method, would He have done so? One hardly needs to read the New Testament extensively to get the answer. No, He would not have saved us in such a way.

Jesus Christ could not have endured the thought of a salvation that left a stain on the character of God. Better that all men perish for ever than that men be saved without displaying the justice of God! *And why is this so? Because Jesus Christ loved the beauty of the character of God.* Christ's death was an act of worship, a tribute to the surpassing wonder of God's holiness. If we do not see His death in this light we miss a chief point in His dying. *Justice* demanded His death when He became the sinner's substitute! But that is not all. There is this also: Jesus loved God's justice as He loved all else that belonged to the character of God, His Father.

That does not mean, however, that we ought to forget Christ's love for sinners. Not at all! As the *God*-man the Lord Jesus shares the love and compassion that God has for lost men. As the God-*man* He feels the pity and mercy that every man would feel for every other man if sin had not robbed us of our primitive humanity. Both of these things are true. Each of these expressions of love beat in the heart of Jesus Christ.

Right here I must guard against a common misunderstanding. There seems to be the idea in the minds of some that God did not love men until Jesus somehow brought Him to do so. If that had been the case it would not be right for me to speak of 'the love and compassion God has for lost men'. Not then, at least. At that point, there would have been no such love to talk about. The false scheme takes this form. God was full of hatred toward sinners. If He had had His way He would have destroyed us all. But then the Lord Jesus intervened. By His death upon the cross He turned God's hatred for sinners into love for sinners.

I want you to see that this view of things is wrong throughout. Everywhere there is the closest harmony between the Father and the Lord Jesus. They simply do not clash. It is unthinkable. We may see this clearly in what is perhaps the best-loved verse in the Bible, *John 3:16*:

> For God so loved the world that he gave his one and only Son, that whoever believes in him shall not perish but have eternal life.

Here it is plain that Christ's mission is the work of God. And that verse does not by any means stand alone. Listen to this:

> This is how God showed his love among us: He sent his one and only Son into the world that we might live through him. This is love: not that we loved God, but that he loved us and sent his Son as an atoning sacrifice for our sins (*I John 4:9, 10*).

The truth of these verses is this: The Father and the Son are at one in the salvation of sinful men. Love for sinners proceeds from the very heart of God.

And there is one thing more. The Lord Jesus loves fallen men because He Himself is a man. As a man He has pity and compassion because He is the perfect man, the man who is what all men should be, and would have been, apart from the Fall. Sin is a thief. It has robbed us of the love that God first planted in the heart of man. But it has not robbed Jesus. It is clear that we must love God with all our being. That is still God's prime demand. But Jesus said there is a second command that is like it: 'Love your neighbor as yourself' (*Matthew 22:39*).

Now we have not done these things, but Jesus has. And in doing that second thing – loving His neighbor – the Lord Jesus has kept nothing back. He once said, 'Greater love has no one than this, that one lay down his life for his friends' (*John 15:13*). These were not mere pious words with Jesus. In themselves they were true words. They would have been true if He had simply said them and passed on to some other task. But Jesus did much more than that. He went on to show what they meant in the costliest way possible. He died for His friends. Love sent Jesus to the cross, love as God and love as man. At the cross love bought the right to say: 'Come to Me . . . as Savior. Come to Me . . . for forgiveness'.

There is pardon with Jesus Christ; it arises from His love. It is already purchased for all who shall ever come to Him.

Will you come? Be encouraged to do so by the promises of Scripture to repentant and believing sinners. Here are typical examples:

> Let the wicked forsake his way and the evil man his thoughts. Let him turn to the Lord . . . for he will freely pardon (*Isaiah 55:7*).
> I will forgive all their sins of rebellion against me (*Jeremiah 33:8*).
> Take heart, son; your sins are forgiven (*Matthew 9:2*).
> The son of Man has authority on earth to forgive sins (*Mark 2:10*).
> Jesus said to her, 'Your sins are forgiven' (*Luke 7:47*).
> If we confess our sins, he is faithful and just and will forgive us our sins (*I John 1:9*).

5: *Come to Me . . . as Lord*

Since we are guilty the Lord Jesus invites us to come to Himself. When we come He pardons our sins; He forgives us. That is the place where you must start if you hope to be a Christian. But you must not stop there; that is only the beginning. Let me remind you again that it is to Jesus the person you must come, and not simply to one of His functions. Is He the one who forgives sin? Yes, He is, and you must never forget it. But the Lord Jesus is much more than that, and you are to take Him as He is. That is why you must hear Him saying, 'Come to Me . . . as Lord'.

Just now I picked up my dictionary and looked up the word 'lord'. Here is what I found:

1. a person having great power and authority; ruler; master.

I wanted to consult the dictionary definition in order to see how the word 'lord' is most commonly used. And there we have it. A lord is a master or ruler. We might also use more familiar language: a lord is a boss.

Does the Bible mean more than this when it calls Jesus 'Lord'? Yes, it does. Quite often it is another way of saying that Jesus is God. Among the Jews there was great reluctance to use God's name. One way in which they avoided using it was by substituting the word 'Lord' when they met the name of God in the Scriptures. In that way 'Lord', *when it was used in a religious sense*, came to be a synonym for God. So, when someone confessed that

'Jesus is Lord', he acknowledged that Jesus was more than a man. He confessed that Jesus was God.

But this does not mean that we may forget the more common uses of 'lord'. To say that Jesus is God can only be meaningful if the word 'God' has some content. And as soon as we think about the meaning of the word 'God' we are right back with those ideas of ruler and master. God is, as the dictionary says, 'A person having great power and authority'.

If you think about it for a minute you will realise that most of God's power has been exercised without any willingness at all on my part or yours. Whom did God consult in making the worlds? Not me, not you; that is unthinkable. We did not exist, nor did any other persons exist apart from God. In addition, God sustains these worlds. He does it moment by moment. Yet He does not ask us to do anything about it. God does it, and that is that.

We may see this freedom of God in our own lives. He chose that we would exist and where we would be born. He chose our parents and our race. God did all of this without conferring with us in any way. He just did it. We would have done things differently, but He did not consult with us.

Not all of God's lordship, however, is carried on in this way. When Jesus invites a man to come to Him and to take on His yoke He is offering to rule that man in a different way. The larger reign of God, in which God keeps the worlds in motion and arranges the circumstances of men, ever continues. Nothing can turn it from its course. But when the Lord Jesus calls you to Himself He goes a step further. He invites you to come under His *moral* lordship. That means that He will bind Himself to destroy the corruption that I have spoken of as one of the barriers that keep you from God.

Now, of course, some men say 'No' to this invitation. They do not want to part with their sins; rather, they want to nourish them and cherish them. But such men cannot be said to trust Jesus Christ, for to trust the Lord Jesus is to believe that it is good for me to have my sins torn from my embrace even if it should cost me my life. To rely on Christ for forgiveness, without relying on Him to deal with the evil within me, is not to believe in the real Christ who offers Himself to me. It is to have faith in a savior who does not exist. The genuine Lord Jesus works cleansing in the men He pardons and pardons the men whom He cleanses.

But I must enter into more detail at this point. To begin with, what I have already said does not mean that Christ cleanses us all at once. No, you must not take me to mean that! It does mean, however, that at the moment we are forgiven the work of being made holy is started. And we are in for the whole course! Our cleansing will take the rest of our lives. For reasons that satisfy God He has not chosen to do the thing in an instant. Our 'sanctification' (to use the theologian's word) goes on through thick and thin until He calls us home.

Neither should you suppose that the Lord Jesus puts off our forgiveness to some future day when we are all that we ought to be. Thank God that is not the case! When a man comes to Christ God forgives his sin there and then. And not a part of it either, but all of it! God says, 'Their sins and lawless acts I will remember no more' (*Hebrews 10:17*). These two things, the forgiveness of my sins and my sanctification, go hand in hand. Neither exists without the other. Both are the work of Christ.

I think I see the reason why God forgives the believer's sins at the outset of the Christian life. Quite frankly, the Christian life is a struggle. It is a warfare. It is not easy; it is tough. You must not let this fact discourage you from turning to Christ, but fact it is. Christianity is not for the weak-kneed, the faint-hearted. But, of course, the spectre of unforgiven sin is one of the things that makes all aspects of life difficult. It is one of the things that weakens our knees and makes our hearts faint.

Earlier I showed you two uses of the word 'guilt'. One was: liability to punishment. In that sense a man may be guilty and not even know it. And in that way we are all guilty before God, whether we feel anything about it or not. We are liable for punishment because we have not worshipped and served our Creator, our God. Now when God forgives our sins He takes away that liability to be punished. We are free from the guilt of our sins. What a blessed freedom that is!

But that is not all. 'Guilt' also refers to our feelings. We are said to have 'guilt feelings' when we feel uneasy about the things we have done. We feel 'guilt' when we fear that a punishment we justly deserve will fall upon us. That is likely to mean this: as long as we feel guilty we shall not be able to serve God with heart and soul and mind and strength. So then, in forgiving our sins and in telling us about it, God is setting the stage for us to serve Him with enthusiasm. He is aiding us in following Christ as our Lord.

What I want to do now is this. I want to help you to see what it will mean for you to come to Christ as your ruler or master. I hope to show you just how the Scriptures lead us to understand the lordship of Jesus. I have three things in mind here. They are:

(1) Jesus Christ as the Lord of your principles.
(2) Jesus Christ as the Lord of your actions.
(3) Jesus Christ as the Lord of your opinions.

By 'principles' I mean the general rules we live by. I have inserted the word 'general' in my definition because I am thinking of those rules that cover many situations. If one of your principles, for instance, is to be honest you will have reason to apply that principle in all kinds of circumstances.

When the Lord Jesus urges you to come to Him as Lord He means that you are to adopt the principles He lays down in His word. That is the first thing. You may not claim to be His follower unless you mean to take up His principles.

I want to illustrate this by a story from Jesus' life. Early in His ministry Jesus called Matthew to follow Him. From the viewpoint of the 'best' people Matthew was an undesirable convert. He was a tax collector. Tax collectors in Jesus' day were hated men. It was not simply that they collected taxes. That was bad enough, but that was not all. They were shunned by society chiefly because they were looked on as agents of a foreign ruler. The people of Israel were very much under the heel of Rome, but they despised Roman rule. And they had no stomach for those who worked for Caesar.

After Matthew had heard the Savior's call and followed Him, he invited Jesus to dinner. And Jesus went.

> While Jesus was having dinner at Matthew's house, many tax collectors and 'sinners' came and ate with him and his disciples. When the Pharisees saw this, they asked his disciples, 'Why does your teacher eat with tax collectors and "sinners"?'
>
> On hearing this, Jesus said, 'It is not the healthy who need a doctor, but the sick. But go and learn what this means: "I desire mercy, not sacrifice." For I have not come to call the righteous, but sinners' (*Matthew 9:10–13*).

Take another look at the words, 'I desire mercy, and not sacrifice', words that Jesus quoted from the Old Testament. God had said those words to men who had regularly given offerings to God. And that was good; they were supposed to do so. Yet, in spite of their giving, God was displeased. Was God being unreasonable? Let us see.

In the Bible God makes one point over and over again. It is this. Religious observances – for example, prayers, giving money, and attending the church meetings – have no value of their own. God is only pleased with them when something else goes along with them. That 'something else' is mercy or love. It is not that praying and giving and attending meetings are not good things to do. They are, but if they are not accompanied by mercy and love, they may look substantial but they are hollow. They are empty. Worse than that, they offend God.

Now notice how Jesus applied all this to His own critics. He said to them, in effect, 'It is a set habit with you to offer sacrifices. You wouldn't miss doing that. You know when it ought to be done, and you do it. But you Pharisees have missed something. You lack love. You look down your noses at tax collectors and others who do not fit your mould.' Then Jesus added, 'Get out of here! And don't come back until you have learned about mercy and love!'

I tremble to think of the Lord Jesus telling anyone to go away. Yet that is what He did. In doing that He claimed to be Lord over the Pharisees' principles. If they would not adopt His godly principles, Jesus would have nothing to do with them. If they would not repent, He would distance Himself from them – for ever!

And that is the way it is with you also. Jesus Christ will be Lord of your principles. Of course, it will take the rest of your life to learn what all those principles are. I cannot promise you a short course. I am still in this school myself. And I have a long way to go. But still, you and I must be enrolled if we are to think of ourselves as Christians. The trouble with the Pharisees was not only their ignorance.

We are all ignorant to an appalling degree. Their problem was that they would not become learners. They sneered at becoming Jesus' pupils. They would not enroll as His disciples. They did not 'believe in Him' and had no desire that He should be their teacher.

I can make this point another way by calling the Lord Jesus' school a 'vocational school'. Some schools are what we might call 'academic schools'. Boys and girls and men and women may go to those schools without at all aiming to use what they learn. They may go to 'fulfill themselves', as we say, or for the sheer love of learning. But a vocational school is different. By and large, people go to a vocational school with one end in view. They want to apply what they learn. Their time in school is not just academic, it is practical. They have the rest of their lives in their minds' eye.

Now the Pharisees were fascinated by Jesus. They watched everything He did. They could have told you a great deal more of what He said than I can. But their aim was wrong. They were not about to apply the teaching of Jesus to their lives. To them, His teaching was purely academic. They had no intention of practising it.

And that is the danger we all face. You too, perhaps, are fascinated by Jesus. I hope you are. That comes first, but that is not the main thing. The heart of the matter is this: will Jesus Christ be the Lord of your principles? Is that the way it will be with you from now on? Do not misunderstand me. I am not asking for any guarantees. No, you are far too weak and sinful for that! I am asking about your intention right now. At this moment! Are you ready to start with His principles? With your eye on them, can you say from the heart, 'Jesus Christ is my Lord!'?

In a way, I might stop right here and not go on to speak of Jesus Christ as the Lord of your actions. A man who seeks to live by the principles that Christ lays down in His word will see to it that those principles work out in his acts. That is as sure as anything can be. What we do is the litmus test of the principles we hold. There is one important reason, however, for looking at actions separately. I want to take that up next.

In the Old Testament God tested the obedience of the people of Israel in a peculiar way. What He did was this. He laid down a large number of rules for which we can cite no reason, with utter certainty, even today. Take the food laws, for example. Was it really wrong to eat the flesh of hogs? Yes, it was wrong for an Israelite. But it might have been hard for him to tell you why. 'God commanded it!' – that may have been all he could have said.

In New Testament times God has chosen another way. Now Christians have few rules that are not explained to us in God's word. We have few rituals – almost none, compared to the ceremonies of the Old Testament. We have an enviable liberty. But I must add one caution. It is this. Jesus Christ remains the Lord of our actions. If you are to be a Christian He must be the Lord of your actions as well. That means that when you come upon His commands in Scripture you will obey them. There may be times when the principle that lies behind His command will elude you, but you will obey. God humbles us by our ignorance; He sends us back to His word.

And that brings me to my last point: Christ as the Lord of your opinions. Life in the world is filled with difficult questions and clever answers. As I write, issues of the day include such matters as abortion, nuclear war, women's rights, and the economic rights of undeveloped nations. These questions and a host of others like them are likely to confront us for years to come. They will not go away. What, then, is a Christian to think? The obvious answer is the right one. A Christian is to seek to think whatever Christ thinks about these various matters.

But here is the catch. When you come to Christ you are probably prepared to change your actions. It is usually taken for granted, I think, that a person who becomes a Christian will have to give up some of his old ways. That seems to be a 'given' that is recognised all around. I am not so sure that the same thing can be said of our opinions. I believe very few of us who have come to Christ started with the conviction that we needed a new set of opinions about the pressing problems of our age and of our lives. At least I did not.

The day you turn to Christ you will not know which of your cherished ideas will have to go. You cannot know that at the outset. It is impossible. But you may be sure of this. Jesus Christ will extend His lordship to all of life. And if you trust Him, you will trust His wisdom. It will not be a matter of gratitude. You will not say to yourself, 'Christ has forgiven my sin, and therefore I owe it to Him to think as He does'. The human mind will not work that way. No amount of gratitude will make you adopt another person's point of view. But something else will. If you trust in Jesus Christ you will recognise His wisdom for what it is, the wisdom of God. Then it will not seem strange for you to take Him as Lord of your opinions. Rather, it will seem absurd to do anything else.

His wisdom is for all who ever come to Him as Lord. Will you come?

6: *Come to Me . . . as Sustainer*

Thus far in this book I have urged you to believe in Jesus Christ. I have told you what 'believing in Christ' means. It means to trust Him comprehensively. The call of Christ is not simply to trust Him to do this or that for you. It is much larger. It is a call to trust all that He is, with all that you are.

At the same time I have tried to focus your attention on two things. One is Christ's conferment of forgiveness upon all who repent and believe the gospel; the other is His promise to be your Lord. Without looking at specific facets of Christ's work we might end up with a sort of sentimental attachment to Jesus that would fall far short of biblical faith. That is not what we are after. It is not possible to trust a person about whom we have only vague ideas.

But trust in Christ would soon come to nothing if we did not have something else to rest upon, something that I have not yet mentioned. I am talking about the sustaining power of the Lord Jesus. That is what I must explain to you next.

If you are at all like I am you have had an automobile that would not run. Sometimes a minor adjustment will put the thing right and get it going again. But there are times when some part of its engine has gone radically wrong and a major overhaul is needed. Nothing else will get the job done. A 'wash-and-wax' is not the answer. Either you do the work deep in the inside or you assign it to the scrap heap. It comes down to that.

Now the man without Jesus Christ is like that car. He stands in need of radical change to transform him on the inside. That is the picture I have tried to draw for you all through this book. If you do not yet belong to the Lord Jesus there is an innate rebellion in your heart against the claims of God and it will not be cured by some cosmetic change. The problem goes to the center of your being, and so must the solution. We are looking here at an overhaul and not a minor adjustment.

But here is an odd thing. Once the automobile has been thoroughly repaired it still will not run. The finest motor in the world is useless until something more than mechanical ingenuity is applied to it. It needs fuel, a continuous supply of gasoline or other energy to keep it going. Without that, we may admire it but we cannot use it. In order to run, even a finely-tuned Rolls Royce must have a source of power. And that is the way it is with us. Earlier I told you that you must trust Jesus Christ to have your sin forgiven. I want to repeat that; it is absolutely basic. Then I said that you must turn to Christ as Lord, to set your principles right and your actions; yes, even your opinions. That too is fundamental. But suppose He forgives your sin and begins to assert His lordship, what then? Why then you will need some sustaining power, something to keep you going, some force to keep up your faith when it begins to sink. And for that, also, you must look to Jesus Christ. It begins to look as if you must trust the Lord Jesus for everything. And that is it – that is the whole point of Christianity!

A few minutes ago I read of a man who was said to have had 'occasional fits of devout feeling'. What a descriptive phrase! How like most of us that is, apart from God's grace! But when Jesus Christ takes hold of us, everything changes. He has promised to sustain His people, and He calls on us to trust Him to do so. Let us try to see what that means.

Here are words Jesus said to His friends the night before He was killed.

> If you love me, you will obey what I command. I will ask the Father, and he will give you another Counselor to be with you for ever – the Spirit of truth . . . I will not leave you as orphans; I will come to you (*John 14: 15–18*).

These words introduce us to a new power, the One called in Scripture 'the Holy Spirit'. Jesus spoke of the Spirit to offset the fears of His followers when they grasped the fact that He was going to leave them. They thought that if He were to go away all their hopes would be crushed. 'Not so!' said Jesus. 'Not at all!' Later that evening the Lord Jesus added,

> It is for your good that I am going away. Unless I go away, the Counselor will not come to you; but if I go, I will send him to you (*John 16:7*).

The coming of the Spirit was of first importance to the disciples, although just then they could not have told you why.

The reason was this. To this point in their Christian lives the disciples had depended upon the Lord Jesus to empower them. Jesus encouraged them and instructed them and counseled them and rebuked them when they needed it. They drew upon His wisdom and guidance to keep them going. His presence and ministry to them was the fuel for their own efforts. They could not imagine life without Him. It was unthinkable.

Now here is what is important. These disciples were right in thinking they could not live without the Lord Jesus. This was not a case of mere sentimentality. It struck far deeper than that. Their understanding was sound. They must have the Lord Jesus or die spiritually. It was as simple as that! Yet there He was, telling them to bid Him goodbye. Or so it seemed.

But the all-important fact was this: the Spirit, who was to come, was God also. Just as Jesus Christ is God, so the Holy Spirit is God. Yet while the friends of Jesus could no longer have His physical presence, they still needed His wisdom and guidance. They wanted the refreshment that His counsel had brought them. And these things the Spirit of God would give. The Spirit would take the place of Jesus as the helper of His friends. He would be 'another Jesus'! He would not be with them visibly as Jesus had been, but He would live within them, 'the Spirit of truth' (*John 14:16–17*).

Now you must not think of this simply as history. It *is* history, of course. Jesus' first-century followers found that the Spirit came to them and supplied the place that the Lord Jesus had held among them. All of that is true. But what interests us is this: it happens today. In every age since the Lord Jesus returned to His Father in heaven, He has given His Spirit to His people. The gift of the Spirit sustains us. And, if you come to Christ, He will sustain you as well.

The Bible gives us two answers when we ask the question, 'What is it that the Spirit does for believers?' We might call these 'an outside answer' and 'an inside answer'. By 'an outside answer' I mean that the Spirit has done something outside of us to help us greatly. I am thinking of His work in producing the Scriptures. Of course, that was a once-for-all work. I want to take it up later. Just now, however, it is the 'inside answer' on which I want to focus. A major part of the Spirit's work is within the believer. There He plants an inclination to obey and follow the teaching of the Scriptures that He has produced. This 'inside' work necessarily goes on through all the Christian's life. It is this that sustains him.

In the last chapter I told you that Jesus will assert His lordship over your life if you become a Christian. That is certainly true; He does it with all who follow Him. I do not know what kind of vision that fact raised in your mind. Perhaps none at all. But it is just possible that I led you to think of the Lord Jesus as working against your own inclinations and crushing you into submission. That is not the case. The truth is far different.

The Lord Jesus asserts His lordship by sending His Spirit. It is the Spirit's work to give us a love for the ways of Christ. It is not a question of continually beating back the Christian's desires. There is no forcing the believer to be what he should be. That is not how God works. For one thing, there would be no end to that task. If we were not changed inwardly we would need to be pushed along throughout eternity. But that is not the picture the Bible gives us. Not at all!

The Spirit forms our attitudes; that is the main thing. It is not that actions are unimportant. We dare not ignore them. But attitudes lie behind sincere actions, so that is where the Spirit goes to work. Paul shows us the result in his letter to the Galatians.

> The fruit of the Spirit is love, joy, peace, patience, kindness, goodness, faithfulness, gentleness and self-control (*Galatians 5:22, 23*).

You do not get such 'fruit' by applying physical force. Love, joy, peace and the rest lie at the heart of what a man is. You must change the person to grow this fruit, and in this work the Spirit is continually engaged. We are commanded to have these fruits, these attitudes, in the Scriptures. And, as I have said, these same Scriptures were themselves produced by the Spirit. But He does not simply leave us with His commands. If we are Christians the Spirit gives us the desire to obey Him. In that way

He makes these attitudes our own. His word outside us and His work within us go hand in hand. And, remember, this work of the Spirit is Jesus Christ's gift to us. It is His way of sustaining us and supporting us as we follow Him.

Before I close this chapter let me try to bring its point home to you once more. I have in mind some words of Jesus that have never been popular. But we must hear them. They are for our good.

> Suppose one of you wants to build a tower. Will he not first sit down and estimate the cost to see if he has enough money to complete it? For if he lays the foundation and is not able to finish it, everyone who sees it will ridicule him, saying, 'This fellow began to build and was not able to finish.'
>
> Or suppose a king is about to go to war against another king. Will he not first sit down and consider whether he is able with ten thousand men to oppose the one coming against him with twenty thousand? If he is not able, he will send a delegation while the other is still a long way off and will ask for terms of peace. *In the same way, any of you who does not give up everything he has cannot be my disciple* (*Luke 14:28–33*).

These are sobering words. Let us see if we can understand them.

Jesus' subject is the high cost of discipleship. In words I have put in italics the Lord speaks plainly: to follow Him will cost us everything. He could not have made a greater demand. No wonder these words are not popular! How could they be?

But suppose you mean to take these words seriously. What then? These stories of Jesus speak not only of high cost but of resources. The builder has money. The king has soldiers. But what resources has the man who wants to be a Christian? Scripture's answer is this: he has none!

And that brings me to my point. Suppose you come to Christ with the intention of following Him, of forsaking all for His sake. No one could fault you for that. That is the only attitude to take when you turn to Jesus. But that raises some questions. What hope do you have for the future? How will you feel about serving Christ a week from now? A month from now? Five years from now? What will happen then?

There is a pitfall here. The danger is that you will call in your self-confidence to answer these questions. In the heat of the moment you may feel that all will go smoothly because of the strength of your present convictions. You – of all people – will not turn back!

But over against this kind of self-confidence you must set confidence in Christ. It is better to enter into the Christian life with fear and trembling than to suppose that the strength of today's determination will carry you through. Note this carefully: *To look to yourself to sustain yourself is a kind of idolatry*. It is self-worship. It is to imagine that you have resources that you do not have. Let me say it again: it would be better for you to start the Christian life with dread of failure than it would be to look to your own power to sustain you in living the Christian life.

But, thanks be to God, you need not do either of these things. In fact, you must not! The same Jesus Christ, who promises to forgive you and to be your Lord, promises to sustain you. He will not do one without the others. He will do all three if you come to Him.

I have no doubt what Christ will do if you come to Him. That is settled in my mind. But will you come? Let me press these questions upon you. Do you have sins that need forgiving, or do you not? Do you need a Lord to lead you in the service of God, or do you not? And do you require Someone to sustain you who is more than man, or do you not? On your answer to these questions hangs your eternal destiny. May God give you grace to answer them wisely!

7: Come to Me . . . as Teacher

Christianity thrives on knowledge. That is not always understood, but it is true. Christianity is not mysticism. It does not seek to deny reason. It does not try to produce experiences that are wholly outside our mental processes. In fact, it does the opposite. It aims to inform the mind. *The Christian life is lived on facts.*

I may illustrate this by reminding you what this book is like. What I have been doing is telling you truths. I have brought up facts about God and about yourself, facts found in the Scriptures. I started to say that I have deliberately avoided any talk about trances or self-hypnosis or anything else that might induce some kind of experience that bypasses the mind. But the truth is that I have not 'deliberately avoided' that approach. It did not occur to me. It would not occur to any man who takes the Bible for what it professes to be. Like every other book it has a character of its own. And 'mystical' is not the word to describe it. That is not to say that no man who has been called a 'mystic' was a Christian. No, I would not want to say that. But it is to say that the center of Christianity is elsewhere. It does not lie in any process that disengages the mind. You will need your wits about you at all times if you hope to be a Christian. The appeal to reason is found everywhere in Scripture. Here, for example, is a word God gave through an Old Testament prophet. He appeals to men like ourselves to turn from sin and to seek forgiveness.

> 'Come now, let us *reason* together,' says the Lord. 'though your sins are like scarlet, they shall be as white as snow; though they are red as crimson, they shall be like wool' (*Isaiah 1:18*).

In the New Testament we find the same emphasis. Here are words of Christ Himself:

> Man does not live on bread alone, but on every word that comes from the mouth of God (*Matthew 4:4*).

That is, man must hear and understand what God has to say. Then he can 'live'. Otherwise, what he goes through will be a kind of walking death. Truth alone can keep him alive.

I do not want to labor this point, but you can easily check the matter for yourself. Turn over the pages of the Bible. Note how much of it is history, for instance. Over half the New Testament is the story of Christ and the early church. That is history. And notice something else too. There is little or nothing in it to induce an unusual emotional or psychological state of mind. Even its hymns are brimming with facts about God and His works.

What are we to think about this? It is not hard to answer that question, is it? It seems clear that God is telling us that our minds need to be taught. And one other thing seems plain also. Judging from the size and contents of the Bible, we need very much more instruction than we would have thought possible. That goes for me, and that goes for you too.

Now in the Bible Christ is our teacher, especially in the New Testament. As we have seen, when He sent the Holy Spirit to His church Jesus had two things in mind. First, He wanted the Spirit to produce the New Testament. Second, He sent the Spirit to give us the inclination to follow it. The Spirit, of course, has done both these things. We now have the New Testament. And if we are

Christians – even feeble ones – the Spirit has begun to move us to do the will of Christ as we find it in His word.

How does the Lord Jesus Christ teach the man or woman who comes to Him? He has many ways of doing that. I want to take them up in the rest of this chapter. To make a start we will need to look at two of the most important: Jesus' own words, and His character while He was here on earth. For the most part the first four books of the New Testament, called the Gospels, will be our source.

First, let me show you what value Jesus attached to His own words. We have seen His statement about God's words. Here is His verdict on His own sayings:

> Therefore everyone who hears these words of mine and puts them into practice is like a wise man who built his house on the rock. The rain came down, the streams rose, and the winds blew and beat against that house; yet it did not fall, because it had its foundation on the rock.
>
> But everyone who hears these words of mine and does not put them into practice is like a foolish man who built his house on sand. The rain came down, the streams rose, and the winds blew and beat against that house, and it fell with a great crash (*Matthew 7:24–27*).

These words are plain enough. They show that Jesus thought His own teaching was greatly important. Once He told us that men must live by God's words; here He says the same of His own. Make His teaching the foundation of your life and succeed. Or, ignore it and fail. Those are the choices. It would be hard to make a higher claim than that. But again Christ says, 'Heaven and earth will pass away, but my words will never pass away' (*Matthew 24:35*).

Now suppose that one of us were to talk in this way. It would sound quite ridiculous, would it not? For one thing there would be a jar and a clash between our lofty words and what any bystander could see us to be. The whole thing would be absurd. It is not that Jesus' words are impossible. That is not the problem. It is just that it takes a man of the Lord Jesus' stature to make them believable. For this reason, hearing Christ's words has always led men who have taken them seriously to examine His person too. And this, in turn, has brought them to learn from what they have seen Him to be. Jesus teaches us by His character as well as by His words. What He is backs up what He says.

Let us start with the things Jesus says about how we ought to act. We like this test best when it is not being applied to ourselves because we know how it is likely to turn out. Let a man tell us all the ways in which we need to improve and we are pretty sure what will happen next. Sooner or later – and generally sooner rather than later – he will trip up. And when this happens, we are ready to gloat over his failure and to excuse ourselves from following his advice, even if it is sound. Somehow we manage to think that the fall of others relieves us of much of our own duty.

But what happens when we apply this test to Jesus? Let us see. Here is one of His commands to us.

> You have heard that it was said, 'Love your neighbor and hate your enemy'. But I tell you: Love your enemies and pray for those who persecute you, that you may be sons of your Father in heaven (*Matthew 5:43–45*).

How will our Lord stand the trial of His own words?

First, listen to Peter telling of Jesus' conduct on the cross:

> Christ suffered for you, leaving you an example, that you should follow in his steps . . . When they hurled their insults at him, he did not retaliate; when he suffered, he made no threats. Instead, he entrusted himself to him who judges justly (*1 Peter 2:21, 23*).

And that is not all. Keeping in mind Jesus' words about praying for our persecutors, listen to this:

> When they came to the place called The Skull, there they crucified him, along with the criminals – one on his right, the other on his left. *Jesus said, 'Father, forgive them, for they do not know what they are doing'* (*Luke 23:33, 34*).

It is true, of course, that to teach us how to act was not the main thing Jesus had in mind when He prayed for His persecutors. His prayer shows us what He was like much more than it tells us what He wants us to be like. But that does not keep us from profiting from His example. It teaches us. It rebukes us. And it does it in the best way possible. Now we *see* what praying for those who hate us means. We can no longer say we do not know.

But the cross – or rather, Jesus on the cross – has more truth to give us. Let me take up another point. We do not like the theme of judgment. It reminds us that we are not gods. We are answerable to the One who made us. We prefer a cheerier note, but the word 'judgment' was often on the Lord Jesus' lips. Once some of His listeners told Him of a disaster in Galilee that cost many lives. Here is Jesus' response:

> Do you think that these Galileans were worse sinners than all the other Galileans because they suffered this way? I tell you, no! But unless you repent, you too will all perish (*Luke 13:2, 3*).

Then He reminded them of another calamity.

> Those eighteen who died when the tower in Siloam fell on them – do you think they were more guilty than all the others living in Jerusalem? I tell you, no! But unless you repent, you too will all perish (*Luke 13:4,5*).

Now here is the thing to notice. If someone were to ask how much weight he should give to Jesus' talk about God's judgment on sin, the cross is the answer. I would have to say what I said before. To teach us that His words about judgment were true was not the main thing Jesus had in mind in dying. Besides, even if we knew nothing of the cross, we ought to believe the words of the Lord Jesus on judgment as on every other theme. But the cross is a tool to teach us. Christ's death makes it clear that God has not lost His will to judge sin. That is what the cross is about. The killing of Jesus was no accident. Not at all! In the cross we see our Savior receiving the punishment due to all who shall ever trust Him. In that way Jesus teaches us from the cross, even as He dies for sinners. In the midst of His agony He says to *you*, 'Come to Me . . . as Teacher!'

We must not think that when we move on from the story of Jesus' life on earth we also leave His teaching. It is still Christ who is teaching us when we read in the New Testament of the early church. That story is full of good things. And we have it because Christ, by His Spirit, moved men to write it down accurately. You may read that account in the book of Acts.

But I want to go a step further. Not all of the New Testament is history. It is all, however, the teaching of Christ. That goes for what is called 'theology' as well. Theology is the study of God and His relation to the things He has made. If we look at the theology of the cross, then, we are paying attention to what God was doing at the cross. The meaning of the cross is the theology of the cross. We must not let the word 'theology' scare us.

In trying to show you the meaning of the cross, I was teaching you theology. But how can I know what God was doing when He sent His Son to die? One answer is found in the Gospels themselves. The Gospels give me hints and glimpses of what Christ has done on the cross. But there is a fuller source for the meaning of the cross, namely, the letters of Paul and others in the New Testament. These letters are also the work of the Spirit that Jesus sent. In that way Jesus Himself is still teaching us.

Christ's early followers, men like Paul, knew that their teaching was not their own. It was Christ's. Paul makes that clear in this passage:

> We are therefore Christ's ambassadors, as though God were making his appeal through us. We implore you on Christ's behalf: Be reconciled to God (*2 Corinthians 5:20*).

An ambassador has no message of his own. He is not told to be original. His job is to speak the words of another. In Paul's case, the words were Christ's. That means that if you come to Christ as Teacher, you will often find yourself pondering more than you read in the Gospels. All the words of the New Testament are His. You will need every one of them.

And now I am nearly done with this chapter. There is one more thing, however, that I must take up, the teaching of Christ that helps us look to the future. Make no mistake about it: a Christian has his eye on eternity. That is no accident. The Lord Jesus planned it that way.

But do not misunderstand me. I am not about to give you a detailed timetable of future events. I really could not do that, and it is not what you need. What I want to do is both easier and harder than to supply a timetable. My aim is to help you to get an attitude. It is much easier to explain the Christian attitude toward the future than it would be to tell you everything that lies ahead. On the other hand, it will be much harder for you to develop this frame of mind than it would be to memorise a list of future events.

Do you know what 'pie in the sky bye and bye' means? Or, 'a bird in the hand is worth two in the bush'? We use both phrases to describe attitudes toward the future. The man who looks for 'pie in the sky' is an impractical chap, or so it is thought. But the world admires the fellow who thinks 'a bird in the hand is worth two in the bush'. He is not a dreamer. He has his feet on the ground. He takes what he can get while he can get it. He is the 'practical' man. Or, at least, that is the popular wisdom.

What often goes unnoticed when we use these phrases is the vast amount that is left unsaid. At the very least we ought to ask a question. 'Why does Smith wait, while Jones grabs what is at hand?' And we ought to insist on an answer. That will tell us who is the wiser man, even when we are dealing with everyday affairs. We will weigh their reasons. The chances are that sometimes Jones will seem to have the clear head. But sometimes it will be Smith, despite the fact that both phrases point to Jones as the man to follow!

To become a Christian means to give up the 'sure thing', 'the bird in the hand'.

Jesus put it this way:

> If anyone would come after me, he must deny himself and take up his cross and follow me. For whoever wants to save his life will lose it, but whoever loses his life for me and for the gospel will save it. What good is it for a man to gain the whole world, yet forfeit his soul? Or what can a man give in exchange for his soul? If anyone is ashamed of me and my words in this adulterous and sinful generation, the Son of Man will be ashamed of him when he comes in his Father's glory with the holy angels (*Mark 8:34–38*).

Jesus' point of view here is clearly future. Today's 'sure things' are not what they seem. That is His message.

Instead, a man needs to lose his life! And then, in a startling figure, He says that throwing away your life for Him and for the gospel is the only way to save it. What does He mean?

The Lord Jesus means two things. First, you are to live your life for God. Use your energy to serve Him and to help spread His word. In a word, *come to Jesus and follow Him, to death if necessary*. That is the chief thing. But if you will not do that, then there is a second thing. You are to remember that Judgment is coming. Then the scramble for position and power and pleasure and money will be seen for what it is. And what is it? It is not life; it never was life. It is a fool's game, the game of death in which a man sells his soul and gets nothing eternal – except hell – in return.

The Lord Jesus stands over against the emptiness of a life without God. And He stands there as Teacher. 'Come to Me', He says. 'Take my yoke upon you and learn from me, for I am gentle and humble in heart, and you will find rest for your souls.' On a later day He added, 'My sheep listen to my voice' (*John 10:27*). Jesus' sheep learn from Him; that is the test. It has tested the resolve of millions of others, and now it tests you. Will you respond as He says, 'Come to Me . . . as Teacher'?

May God help you to say, 'I come!'

8: *Come to Me . . . as King*

In this chapter I shall share something with you that is almost always left out of a book like this. I am sure that many people would say that you are not ready to hear what I hope to give you next. But I cannot agree with them. Let me tell you why.

So far I have urged you to turn to Christ. I have said 'Come to Him' in many different ways. And I am not done yet. But earlier we talked about how you would help me to love and trust a friend of yours. I suggested that you would tell me what your friend is like, how he acts, and what he says. We are more likely to trust someone when we can judge for ourselves whether or not he is trustworthy. Hearing 'Believe, believe, believe in my friend!' is a small part of the process. 'What is your friend like?' – that is the question.

But that raises another question. Would you tell me *all* about your friend? Or, would you keep some things back? That could be a sticky problem. For one thing, we owe it to every man to be quiet about his faults unless we are forced to speak of them. That, of course, is a rule we often break – or, at any rate, a rule *I* often break – but it is a good one nevertheless.

Now you will need to follow me closely here. I am not about to speak of one of the Lord Jesus' faults, for He is 'holy, blameless, pure, set apart from sinners' (*Hebrews 7:26*). But if you have read the New Testament you will know that Jesus' innocence did not keep people from grumbling and complaining against Him. Quite the opposite! They hounded Him, literally, to death. And they felt smugly satisfied in doing it. 'Away with such a fellow!' was their cry.

Can you tell why they did such a thing? The answer, I think, is clear. There was a good deal about Jesus that offended men. There were things that He did and said that infuriated His listeners. And, naturally, they thought the fault was in Him and not in themselves.

One of the things Jesus did is connected with a phrase that Christians have come to use to describe God. That phrase is 'the sovereignty of God'. Sovereignty is kingship. When we speak of the sovereignty of God we mean that God is King, that He rules in the worlds He has made. And, when we leave it at that, no one seems to raise much objection.

But the Lord Jesus applied the idea of God's kingship in an unexpected way. The time arrived when He told His followers that He Himself was about to exercise that kingship in the same way. As God had been spoken of as King, so He would be King. From then on, men stumbled at Jesus as King. They still do. As long as His kingship is a vague notion with little content, many are ready to give Jesus the title. But when He asserts His kingship in the way I am about to describe they are filled with resentment.

Let me put the point as baldly as possible so that you cannot mistake my meaning. What men hated to hear was this: *God saves whom He pleases*. To speak of God's kingship in a general way was one thing, but to apply it to salvation was quite another; in fact it was more than they could bear! Yet Jesus would not retract His teaching. Let men say what they will, still *God saves whom He pleases*. Or, to apply it to Christ, the Lord Jesus, as God, saves those He makes up His mind to save. It is in Christ's hand to deliver us from our sins or to pass us by.

That is one chief thing we mean when we say that Jesus is King.

If you have understood what I said in the last paragraph I am sure that you also feel a difficulty. (If you do not feel it, I urge you to read the paragraph again.) It is one thing to urge men and women to turn to Christ. That seems plain enough. But it is quite another thing to say that whether or not they turn is in the hands of Christ. Surely something is wrong here! Or so it would seem. What use is there in pleading with men to come to Jesus if, in fact, the whole thing is out of their control? Questions like these cry out for an answer when we say that God and Christ save whom They please.

Well, there certainly is something wrong here, but the problem is not with God. Let me see if I can make this clear by building on facts we learned earlier. The first fact is this: man is dead. As we have seen, the natural man – man as he comes into this world – is dead toward God. That means that he is content to be without God. He does not want God to interfere in his life. If you are a natural man you have no desire to serve God for God's own sake. To be sure, you may pray. The natural man prays to further his own ends. He would like to use God. But he does not love God; he hates God. That God should get glory and honor and praise and admiration from His creatures is the last thing the natural man is concerned with. That is evident from the way he exists.

Now put the fact that man is dead with this second truth: God is the Creator of life! Of the things God has created, *life* is the most remarkable. The sun, the moon, the stars – these are fitted to make us wonder at God's wisdom and power. But when we think of *life*, all else pales beside it.

So we have these two things. The human race is dead, and God can give life. But to whom shall He give it? To those who ask? Maybe –. But consider this. If life means seeking the glory of God, serving Him for His own sake, and loving God above all others, including ourselves, we have a problem. Here it is. Who, understanding these things, will ask God for life? Not the natural man! These are the very things from which he runs. He has a simple reason for doing so. To have these attitudes would devastate him; they would destroy his present 'life'! Of course, what he calls 'life' is really death as God sees it. But the natural man cares nothing for God's point of view because he cares nothing for God. That is what we mean when we say that he is dead.

What, then, is the use of addressing the natural man? If he is dead and will not respond, are we not wasting our breath or our paper and ink? Let us see if we can find the answer to these questions.

Imagine that God looked at a group of corpses and that He made up His mind to raise some of them from the dead. How would He go about it? This is not a fanciful question. We know from Scripture that God has in fact already raised a few men and women from the dead. It is clear, I think, that all that is required is an act of God's will. Let God will that they arise and they are certain to come from their graves. Nothing more is absolutely necessary.

It does not follow, however, that God would do it by His bare will alone. He might use some further means. I am not guessing when I speak in this way. We have the examples in the Bible to show us how God works. Jesus Christ, the God-man, will be our teacher.

On three occasions Jesus raised a person from the dead. One was the daughter of a man named Jairus, a synagogue ruler. While Jairus was hoping that the Lord Jesus would come to his house to heal his daughter he received word that she had died. But Jesus said, 'Don't be afraid; just believe.' The New Testament writer, Mark, will tell us what happened next.

> When they came to the home of the synagogue ruler, Jesus saw a commotion, with people crying and wailing loudly . . . . After he put them all out, he took the child's father and mother and the disciples who were with him, and went in where the child was. He took her by the hand and said to her, '*Talitha koum*!' (which means, 'Little girl, I say to you, get up!') Immediately the girl stood up and walked around (she was twelve years old). At this they were completely astonished (*Mark 5:38, 40–42*).

Did Jesus use any means here? Yes, He took the dead girl by the hand, and He spoke to her. Neither would seem to have been necessary, but that is what He did.

A second such raising took place outside the city of Nain.

> As [Jesus] approached the town gate, a dead person was being carried out – the only son of his mother, and she was a widow. And a large crowd from the town was with her. When the Lord saw her, his heart went out to her and he said, 'Don't cry.'
>
> Then he went up and touched the coffin, and those carrying it stood still. He said, 'Young man, I say to you, get up!' The dead man sat up and began to talk, and Jesus gave him back to his mother.
>
> They were all filled with awe and praised God (*Luke 7:12–15*).

What means did Jesus use this time? His word to the young man – that was all!

A third account of Jesus' raising the dead is the story of Lazarus, a member of a family Jesus deeply loved. John tells us what happened when Christ came to the tomb.

It was a cave with a stone laid across the entrance. 'Take away the stone,' he said . . .

So they took away the stone. Then Jesus looked up and said, 'Father, I thank you that you have heard me. I knew that you always hear me, but I said this for the benefit of the people standing here, that they may believe that you sent me.'

When he had said this, Jesus called in a loud voice, 'Lazarus, come out!' The dead man came out . . . Therefore many of the Jews who had come to visit Mary, and had seen what Jesus did, put their faith in him (*John 11:38, 39, 41–45*).

What means did Jesus use here? He 'called in a loud voice, "Lazarus, come out!"'

In each of the three cases Jesus spoke to the dead person. If we did not trust His wisdom we might have an irreverent reaction. After all, what is more useless than to speak to a corpse? But that is what Jesus did, so we want to know His reason. Why did He do this?

The reason is this. The word that God speaks, or that Christ speaks, is a creative word. It not only asks for something to happen; it makes it happen. At the beginning of His creation God said, 'Let there be light'. And light appeared! It was as simple as that! Again, God once spoke of the rain and snow that He sends down from heaven. They water the earth and cause it to yield food. Then God said,

> . . . so is my word that goes out from my mouth: It will not return to me empty, but will accomplish what I desire and achieve the purpose for which I sent it (*Isaiah 55:11*).

Our words may fail, but what God intends, in sending *His* word, is certain to succeed. It will 'accomplish what I desire'. It will achieve His purpose.

We may apply this to the physically dead. Take Lazarus

again. Jesus said, 'Lazarus, come out!' That would have been a useless thing for me to say. My words are not creative. But coming from the God-man those words were full of power. They brought life. 'The dead man came out'. He could do nothing else!

The same thing applies to the spiritually dead. Remember that all men, being sinners, are dead toward God. They do not want God, except to assist them in their own sinful purposes. They do not want 'life' in the biblical sense. The natural man is like a corpse so far as God is concerned. Humanly speaking, his case – and your case, if you are a natural man – is hopeless. You need life. You need a change of heart. You need a new birth!

But 'birth' is in the hands of God. Listen to Jesus on this subject. He is talking with a Pharisee named Nicodemus. He has just told Nicodemus that he and others like him must be 'born again'.

> Flesh gives birth to flesh, but the Spirit gives birth to spirit. You should not be surprised at my saying, 'You must be born again'. The wind blows wherever it pleases. You hear its sound, but you cannot tell where it comes from or where it is going. So it is with everyone born of the Spirit (*John 3:6–8*).

Look at the points Jesus makes here. First He tells us that physical life can only bring forth physical life. To a degree, it is in the power of men and women to have physical children. But no man or woman can bring about spiritual life.

This higher kind of life, this 'new birth' must come from God.

But there is more. In the second place Jesus likens the work of the Spirit to the wind. The wind blows where it pleases. You can see and feel and hear its effects, but there is nothing you can do about it. Even today, with our modern technology, we cannot tell where the molecules that strike our cheek have come from. We do not know where they will go next. In the same way, where God's word is given, the Spirit of God breathes life into men and women as He pleases. The preacher or writer can do nothing about it. The man who is dead spiritually can do nothing about it. It is out of their hands. The life must come from God.

Why then do we tell men and women of Christ and His gospel? Because the Spirit of God uses this message as His instrument. We cannot know when He will use it to save a man, to bring him to a new birth. It is not our business to know before it comes about; it is His business. The Spirit will use this book just as He pleases – whether little or much or not at all. What I can know is this. If you come to Christ through reading this message, your new life will be entirely from God. I will not have produced it in any way. It will be a simple case of God using His message, His word, to raise you from the dead. But if I learn of your conversion I will say the thing the Apostle Peter said:

> For you have been born again, not of perishable seed, but of imperishable, through the living and enduring word of God. For [here he quotes from the Old Testament],
>
> 'All men are like grass, and all their glory is like the flowers of the field; the grass withers and the flowers fall, but the word of the Lord stands for ever.' And this is the word that was preached [and written] to you (*1 Peter 1:23–25*).

So far, then, I have tried to show you the importance of hearing the Word of God. The message concerning Jesus Christ – the gospel – is the means that God uses to bring life. I pray that it may bring life *to you*. That is why I have shared it.

But you might well ask why I have gone to the trouble of telling you that your salvation is in the hands of God. Why did I present the Lord Jesus as King in that sense? I had two reasons for doing so.

The first is this. We men are proud! we like to boast. We like to use William Ernest Henley's words, 'I am the master of my fate: I am the captain of my soul.' That is what we like to do, but that is a delusion. The Bible asserts the opposite. As the sixteenth-century reformer, Martin Luther, put it:

> The Scripture sets before us a man who is not only bound, wretched, captive, sick and dead, but who, through the operation of Satan his lord, adds to his other miseries that of blindness, so that he believes himself to be free, happy, possessed of liberty and ability, whole and alive . . . The work of Satan is to hold men so that they do not recognise their wretchedness, but presume that they can do everything that [God commands].

In a word, Satan seeks to nourish our pride and to keep us blind to our helplessness. But God would humble us. He will humble *you* if He brings you to Christ.

And there is one thing more. All through this book I have told you to look ahead. I have urged you to come to Christ so that, during the rest of your life, you will look to Him as your Savior and Lord and Sustainer and Teacher. But there is something else I want you to do. If you turn to Jesus, from the beginning of your Christian life I want you to look back as well. From the outset I want you to know the meaning of the famous saying: 'There, but for the grace of God, go I!'

The man who knows nothing of his helplessness in the hand of God is in no position to be as thankful as he ought to be when he is brought to Christ. Yes, he may use the words, 'There, but for the grace of God, go I.' But he cannot fully mean them. Instead, he is likely to think of God's grace *plus* his own wisdom or shrewdness or discernment in taking the step of faith. But I do not want that to happen to you.

I urge you again: turn to Christ! But know this. If you come, it will be because Christ is exercising His kingship. So then, come to Christ . . . as King. But when you come, look back. Remember that it was not your power that brought you. It was not your goodness; it was not your wisdom. It was the King Himself! Then, for that reason above all others, praise Him, honor Him, glorify Him and magnify Him for ever.

In doing that you will prove that you have answered His call, 'Come to Me . . . as King'.

9: *Come to Me . . . Exclusively*

Both our eyes and ears play tricks on us. We are told that we see what we expect to see and we hear what we expect to hear. That is one chief reason why communication is difficult. It is hard for me to understand you because I am pretty sure I know what you are going to say. And you have the same problem with me.

All through this book I have been inviting and urging you to come to Christ. Only in Christ is there salvation. It makes sense, then, to abandon all else and to turn to Him. That is the way to be right with God. That is the way to live with God for ever. Come to Christ! Come to Christ alone!

I am afraid, however, that I may be misunderstood. I know that men sometimes misunderstand the message about Christ in the following way. They think they hear the messenger say, 'Add Christ to your church attendance. Add Christ to your baptism. Add Christ to your good works. And *then* God will receive you.' In other words, they suppose that coming to Christ is one item out of many that puts us right with God. But that is not so.

Let us take a glance at church attendance. Is that a good thing? Yes, it is! But can being faithful to the services of the church make you right with God? No, it cannot. Can it help toward God receiving you? No, not in the least. Church attendance can prove you a hypocrite – if you will not come to Christ – but it can do nothing to make you a child of God. Jesus Christ will have all the glory of your salvation, and He will not share it with you because you have been regular in church attendance.

Again, take baptism. Every man, when he becomes a Christian, is commanded to be baptised. Baptism is God's set way of professing faith in Christ. It is a good thing. But God will not receive you because you have been baptised. In fact, just the opposite may be true. God will *refuse to receive you* if you depend on your baptism to save you. Jesus Christ alone can make you right with God, and He will not give you part of the credit because you have been baptised.

That is true of good works as well. Christians are commanded to do good to all men at all times. But Christians are to do good works because they want to please the God who has already received them into friendship with Himself. In other words, they do such works because they *are* Christians. They do not work in order to become Christians. If they depend on their good works to make them right with God they are robbing Jesus Christ of the glory that belongs to Him alone. And a true Christian would never want to do that.

Perhaps I can explain what I mean if we think of the word 'mercy'. Imagine a kind and generous king who has a segment of his people rebel against him. They prove to be no match for the king's troops and shortly they are brought to their knees. They have no excuse for their revolt. They have no defence. What will they do? If they value their lives, they will ask for *mercy*.

Now suppose the king pardons them. Suppose they receive mercy. What then? They will get off scot-free. And will that lead them to serve their king, or will they take his pardon as a licence to rebel again? The truth is, we do not know the answer to that question. But we know what it ought to be! They ought to serve their king for ever, with all their heart.

Let us take the story a little further. Suppose the king has the power to change the hearts of these rebels. Imagine again that he is kind and generous. This time, however, we will add something else about the king. It is this. He has made up his mind that he will never pardon anyone without, at the same time, giving him a heart of gratitude, a bent to please his king. Now we know something we could not guess before. Will his subjects take the king's pardon as a licence to revolt again? Absolutely not!

Such a King is the God of the Bible. He is a God of mercy. He freely pardons. But He does more. When God forgives the sins of any person He also gives that person the desire to serve Him. The service of God's people, however, adds nothing to their pardon. That is free. They are pardoned, one and all, through the merits of Jesus Christ. Their own merit – or lack of it! – has nothing to do with their pardon. Nothing at all! Forgiveness is *mercy*. It is God's mercy, and nothing else.

In this chapter I want you to hear Christ saying, 'Come to Me . . . exclusively'. Let me tell you why. There are two forces that would mislead you when I invite you to Christ. The first is your pride. The second is the pride of others around you.

If you are without Christ you may not want the pardon that Christ offers. Your pride may stand in your way. You may be one of those people who always pays his or her own way. You may say, 'I never take something for nothing!' Many a man has gone to hell with those words on his lips. 'I don't believe in a free ride!' is another way of saying the same thing.

But listen to this. Paul the apostle is speaking of how Abraham was made right with God.

> What does the Scripture say? 'Abraham believed God, and it was credited to him as righteousness.'

> Now when a man works, his wages are not credited to him as a gift, but as an obligation. However, to the man who does not work but trusts God who justifies the wicked, his faith is credited as righteousness (*Romans 4:3–5*).

Notice how Paul drives a man away from his own works. He says that wages earned by work are an obligation. There is no mercy in that. That is not grace. If a man were to work his way with God – that is not possible, you understand – he would have something to boast of. That would minister to his pride. God received me, he would say, because I did such-and-such. O how men like to brag!

But when God humbles you, you will know that you have nothing to give in exchange for pardon. No works, no goodness, nothing at all! Human pride is excluded when God pardons a sinner. To make this plain Paul says, 'God justifies the wicked!' The wicked cannot work their way with God. As Paul put it again: 'Christ died for the ungodly!' (*Romans 5:6*). 'I have not come to call the righteous,' said Jesus, 'but sinners' (*Mark 2:17*). That is another way of saying, 'Come to Me . . . exclusively'. Exclude your own works and (in the process) turn from your own pride!

But you are not yet done. There is still the pride of others to be dealt with. Follow me closely here, because this is a much more subtle danger, but no less real. I am convinced that millions have gone astray at this point without knowing it, until it was for ever too late.

What does the pride of others have to do with your salvation? Just this. When you think you are ready to forsake all credit of your own, other voices will say, 'Give us the credit. We will see that you are saved if you put yourself into our hands. Trust us!' Of course, they will not say, 'Feed our pride instead of your own!' But that is what they will mean.

There are many men who will do this. They will offer to be your spiritual directors. 'Just do as I tell you,' they will say, 'and all will be well.' And then they will impose their rules that are not found in the Word of God. Often their regulations will require a good deal of will-power. They may demand self-sacrifice. But listen to Paul speaking on man-made rules:

> Do not let anyone judge you by what you eat or drink, or with regard to a religious festival, a New Moon celebration or a Sabbath day. These are a shadow of the things that were to come; *the reality, however, is found in Christ* . . . Such regulations indeed have an appearance of wisdom, with their self-imposed worship, their false humility and their harsh treatment of the body, but they lack any value in restraining sensual indulgence (*Colossians 2:16–17, 23*).

Some men love to get other men under their power. There is no quicker way to be thought to be a great leader. There is no surer way to puff up one's ego. But the Scripture will have none of it! Turn to Christ! That is the message! He can do all. None other can do anything. Turn to Him!

There is a further danger from the pride of others. Above I have spoken of individual men who will want you to feed their pride by following their rules. There are many such men. They are everywhere. They have 'seen visions' or 'talked with the Almighty' or have 'tapped the resources within'. They have great appeal. They sound wonderfully spiritual. And you must be on your guard against them. But there is something else, a thing more subtle yet, to watch out for. I have in mind churches and religious groups that will seek to make you depend on them to be right with God. Beware of them – especially!

Let me speak of churches for a moment. If you become a Christian you will need to meet with other Christians in a church or chapel. That is the command of Christ. And, once He has saved you, you will aim to please Him. You will seek the regular fellowship of other believers. That is immensely important. I do not want to make light of it in any way. But you must not do it with your eyes closed. In fact, they must be wide open to the fact that Christ by Himself has made you right with God. How could you think anything else, if you have looked to Jesus Christ alone?

I am sorry to say that not every 'church' has grasped this. A church, for instance, may tell you that you must belong to 'our congregation' or 'our denomination' to be right with God. You will know at once that they are trying to take the place of Christ. Have nothing to do with them!

Watch out for this, too. Will the church make you totally dependent on her sacraments? Will you be denied heaven without them? That is not the church for you! A fellowship that pleases the Lord is known by the fact that her members do not meet to be made right with God *time and again*. Not at all! They gather because Christ has *already* put them right with God. They do not focus on what they can get from the church. That is not the main thing (though they do receive a good deal). They meet to stir one another, to help their brothers and sisters in Christ. And they join to worship. Their meetings are not self-centered. They are centered on others. And – most of all – they are focused on God.

I hope you will notice that what I am talking about is not a matter of style. I am not concerned here to tell you to go to a relatively formal church, or to one that is rather informal. My own bent is toward the less formal type of meeting. But that is not my point at all. I am speaking here of *what the church believes, her doctrines*. Will she put anything but Christ between you and God? Her priests, maybe? Or her ceremonies? Are they necessary to your salvation? Then you must bid her good-bye and go where Christ and Christ alone gets all the glory. This is no longer a matter of taste. The honor of the Lord Jesus is at stake!

A few pages back I was speaking of pride. Since then we have stepped aside to talk of churches. Let me show you how the two are connected. Long ago, before you and I were born, some of these churches were founded. And certain of them were formed by men who wanted credit for making others right with God. They were started by men (or corrupted by men) who wished to tie others to themselves. These men wanted to boast of their power. And they made their doctrines accordingly. Today the doctrines remain. They take away from the glory of Christ. They try to steal the glory of the Christian's salvation from the Lord Jesus. That is the sad fact.

The first question, then, is not, 'How nice are the people at this chapel or church?' Your first question must concern doctrine. It must be about Christ. 'Does this church give Jesus Christ all the glory for the salvation of Christians? Or, does it attempt to share that glory with Him?' The pride of men, long dead, may stand in the way of your trusting in Christ and in Him alone. They may have built dependence on their rites and ceremonies into their systems. And you must run from such systems, into the arms of Jesus Christ!

In closing this chapter I think I hear someone raising another question. It goes like this. 'I thought you were telling me how to come to Christ. Have you not strayed from your theme in speaking of how I ought to choose a church? Are not these quite different things?'

Yes, they are – quite different! But the one illustrates the other. I have been trying to show you the kind of pitfalls I have in mind. It is wise to ponder this carefully. I have been saying that you must come to Christ *exclusively*. If words ever fail to convey my feelings, they do so right here. I wish that, somehow, I might impress you with the enormous importance of this point. I wish I could put you into my own heart for a few seconds and hear it beat, 'Christ alone, Christ alone, Christ alone!'

Men and women everywhere find it easy to turn to a church or religious organisation for salvation. That is far easier than coming to Christ. And so the church becomes a symbol. It is the symbol of all those 'good things' that may keep you from trusting in Christ alone.

'Come to Me', says the Lord Jesus. 'Come to Me . . . exclusively.' Will you turn to Him?

10: Come to Me . . . Immediately

Let me quote the words of the Lord Jesus once more:

> *Come to me, all you who are weary and burdened, and I will give you rest (Matthew 11:28).*

And let me talk with you about the question, 'When shall I come?'

Not long ago I sat in a meeting. The discussion was about telling men of Christ. At one point we turned to the question, 'What do you tell a man who is not ready to repent?' There are many such people. They say 'Yes, I believe what you are telling me is true, but I am not ready yet. One of these days I will be, but not now.' This attitude is so common that we have a proverb to cover it. We say, the road to hell is paved with good intentions.

We might tell such a man any number of things. We could say, 'Read your Bible'. Or, 'Pray!' We could tell him to be faithful in church attendance, to return continually to hear the Word of God preached. We might urge him to talk often with earnest Christians. Yes, we could be tempted to say any of these things, or all of them.

'But wait!' someone says. 'Did you say "*tempted*"? Is not that a strange word to use in this connection?' No, it is not. Let me tell you why I use the word. I will ask you to follow me closely here.

I am always in danger of not dealing with you faithfully. So is every other believer. If you are not a Christian, we are commanded by our Lord to be compassionate toward you.

He has also put that desire in our hearts. We cannot escape it, nor do we want to do so. But if we are not careful we may misuse the very sympathy that God has given us for your good. *We may use it to accept your excuses for not coming to Christ.* If we do that, we are not helping you. We are doing the opposite. We are aiding you to destroy yourself. That is our temptation.

When must you come to Christ? You must come to Him now. Not next week, or next month. You must come now.

Let me remind you of the reason why God created men. He made us to please Him. Whenever God puts a man right with Himself that man begins to seek to please God. That is the first thing God fixes within the newborn Christian. It is the heart of the matter. In that way God shows us that, if we who are men were what we ought to be, we would always seek to please Him. That would be our natural bent. That is what we lost in the Fall. And that is what God restores to us as He re-makes us.

And surely it is plain that we have no right to put off pleasing God! I have no such right, nor do you. Yet 'without faith it is impossible to please God' (*Hebrews 11:6*). You cannot put off pleasing God, and you cannot please Him without turning in faith to Christ! Your duty is plain. You must immediately forsake your sin and, at once, come to the Lord Jesus. I dare not offer you easier terms than these from Scripture: you 'must turn to God in repentance and have faith in our Lord Jesus' (*Acts 20:21*). 'God . . . *now* commands all people everywhere to repent' (*Acts 17:30*).

The Lord Jesus Himself is your example. He needed no repentance, of course. He was the spotless Son of God. But He took pleasing the Father as the great work of His life. That is what gave His life meaning. Once, when He was under fire from His critics, Jesus talked about this main goal:

> When you have lifted up [crucified] the Son of Man, then you will know who I am and that I do nothing on my own but speak just what the Father has taught me. The one who sent me is with me; he has not left me alone, *for I always do what pleases him* (*John 8:28–29*).

Not one of us can say what Jesus said here. No man on earth can make the claim, 'I always do what pleases the Father.' Only Christ could say that. In that way, as in other ways, He was unique. But every Christian can say this: 'Since I have trusted the Lord I have found in myself an increasing desire to serve God. It is often hard. I fail more than I would care to admit. But by degrees I am learning to do His will. I am learning to please God.' That is the point –to please God!

The Christian life is a long journey; it goes on for ever. But like every other trip, long or short, it starts with a first step. For us – sinful people like you and me – repentance and faith are the beginning. And you must set out at once. The hour is already late.

There is another reason why you must turn to Christ *now*. It is this. You are in grave danger of deceiving yourself about the future. If you speak of action 'later', 'later' may never come. It never came for my friend, Roy.

Roy and I worked together at the City Gospel Mission in Cincinnati. Roy was our janitor. But Roy was not a Christian. Of course we often urged him to turn to Christ. And Roy always gave us the same answer.

'I'm not ready just yet,' he would say. 'But I'll tell you this. When I become a Christian I don't intend to be a halfway Christian. When I turn to God I'm going all the way!' And Roy seemed to mean what he said. Looking back, I have no doubt that I took him at his word. But I was wrong, and so was Roy.

Roy fooled himself. Why do I say that? Because – mark it well! – there can never be a good reason for putting off

God. You may put me off for any number of sound reasons. You may sleep upon my proposals. In fact, you must! You would not be a wise man otherwise. But you must not delay, you dare not, when God calls!

I cannot forget the last time I saw Roy alive. He was in General Hospital, or rather on one of its many porches in a wheelchair, for it was a sunshiny day. Another friend and I made small talk with Roy while we waited for the right moment to ask him if he was now ready to turn to Christ. He did not look so bad, but in a few days he would be dead.

The thing that makes that day unforgettable is this. I did not hear Roy say much. He was a severely sick man. But I remember the very last word he said to us. As far as I have been able to make out it was the last word Roy ever spoke to one of his friends. He used it to answer the question we had come to ask. It was the word, 'No'. He did not speak it casually. He did not say it fearfully. It took all the strength he could muster, but he said it defiantly. Just that single word 'No!'

How likely are you to deceive yourself about what you will do in the future? Judge for yourself. Life is a battle in which self-deception plays an immensely important role. That is the kind of fight we are in. Christians, of course, are not the only ones who have seen this. On all hands men cry out against our deceiving ourselves. Some call it 'rationalisation'. Others say, 'That fellow likes to fool himself!' In any case, nothing is held to be more common among us than self-deception.

There is nothing surprising about this when you stop to think of it. It bears out a fact, often repeated in Scripture, that our warfare is over our hearts and minds much more than about how we strike the eye. In the Bible the 'heart' is what the man is, stripped of all mere appearance. As you might guess, the Scriptures say very much about our hearts. Listen to these words:

The heart is deceitful above all things and beyond cure. Who can understand it? I the Lord search the heart and examine the mind . . .

(*Jeremiah 17:9–10*)

Out of the overflow of the heart the mouth speaks.

(*Matthew 12:34*)

Above all else, guard your heart, for it is the wellspring of life.

(*Proverbs 4:23*)

The heart is the thing and, with it, the mind which is its richest part! There the battle rages.

God tells us we are all prone to deceive ourselves. Where, then, can we find help? Well, if we do not understand our own hearts, there is One who does – God Himself. 'I the LORD search the heart and examine the mind.' He is our help. The answer is to hear His words and to trust in Him, and not at all in our own wisdom, not even in our own good intentions. They will let us down, just as they failed Roy.

Let me give you a final reason for turning to Christ without delay: it is for your benefit to do so. I have already suggested many ways in which that is true. Let me point out two more.

First, if you later become a Christian it will grieve you that you put it off so long. Whatever outsiders may think, the service of Jesus gives every Christian true pleasure. And more than one believer has said to himself, 'What a fool I was, that I did not turn to Christ years ago!' It is true that Christianity has also brought us trials. It is not all 'sweetness and light'! But in our saner moments we know that those trials are not to be compared with the smile of our Savior, both here and hereafter.

And if you later become a Christian it will make you sad in another way too. You will think on how ungrateful you were to treat your Savior so. You will be sorry that you spurned His gracious appeal. You will remember that it was your love of sin that made you do so. And the memory may very well break your heart.

Finally, let me speak of the greatest benefit of all. I mean the presence of God. Years ago a group of wise men put together a little question-and-answer book that asks this: 'What is the chief end of man?' As part of their answer they said, 'Man's chief end is . . . to enjoy [God] for ever.' Their answer assumes that eternity will hold enjoyment for every Christian. And so it will! But in what will the enjoyment consist? In the enjoyment of God! That is man's chief end. That is the goal to which Christ will bring us, if we trust Him.

What does it mean 'to enjoy God'? I am sure I cannot say all that it means. That is beyond me. But I have had a glimpse of its meaning. That is what I would like to share with you.

What is the Christian life? In large part it is an increasing understanding of the character of God, of what God is like. And it happens step by step, here a little, there a little, till there is a sense in which we may say, 'I *know* God.' But that is not all. Alongside this there is something else. Some call it 'worship'. It is a special kind of enjoyment.

The Puritan writer, Thomas Watson, urged men to be 'God-admirers'. That was good advice; it still is. And it has this, especially, to commend it: *it is admiration without disappointment, and it is admiration without envy*. When we find men and women whom we admire, our wonder often turns sour. The cause may be in them – 'They let me down!' Or, it may be in us – 'Why should *they* be so talented?' In either case our admiration is ruined, usually for ever!

Over against all this stands the 'enjoyment' of God. It cannot be disappointed, for there are no failures in God to cause disappointment. And it will not make us envious. One of the first effects of seeing God is this: it takes our eyes off ourselves. When I forget 'me!' I can find delight in another. I may look at a fellow human and say, 'Why can't I have his money, or his good looks?' That is common enough, and it may drown our friendship. But let me be awestruck by the Almighty! Then I will forget myself as I am dazzled by the love and mercy and kindness and justice and truth and power of God.

And what is the alternative? What if I do not want God? Let me make it more personal: what if *you* do not come to prize the One who made you? What then?

Jesus said of such a man, 'It would be better for him if he had not been born!' (*Mark 14:21*). Yes, 'better'! That man enjoyed a good deal from the hand of God. His life was not entirely unhappy, perhaps not even largely so. But when Jesus said this He put us all on notice that death is not the end. There is a judgment ahead and, beyond that, for those who reject Him there is hell, an eternity away from God. Listen to these searching words of Christ.

> What good is it for a man to gain the whole world, yet forfeit his soul? Or what can a man give in exchange for his soul? If anyone is ashamed of me and my words in this adulterous and sinful generation, the Son of Man will be ashamed of him when he comes in his Father's glory with the holy angels (*Mark 8:36–38*).

The Son of Man is Jesus. If you do not belong to Him when He comes to judge the world He will disown you for ever. This world's true treasure is not its trinkets. Its lasting treasure is the knowledge of God. And if you trade away the good news of Christ for the world's playthings you will not need another to call you a fool. You will do that for yourself, when it is eternally too late.

Just now, however, you have this moment. Let me borrow the words of a preacher of the last century to tell you what to do with it. Charles Spurgeon said these things in a sermon on Jesus as the friend of sinners:

> In a side street, not far from here, you may have seen in a window this notice, 'If any poor girl upon the streets desires to escape from her sinful way of living, she will find a friend inside.' I felt very pleased when that notice in the window was pointed out to me; and I think that, if I were a poor girl in that sad case, and wished to escape, I should go inside to see what the friend could do for me. The Lord Jesus Christ has put in his window a message of this kind, 'Any sinner of any sort who desires to be saved, let him come to me.' Now, do not merely stand at the window, and read it, but come inside, my poor brother; come inside, my sister. Come to Jesus; come to Jesus just now.

And that is my appeal to you. Come to Jesus; come to Jesus just now. There is no reason to wait outside; there is every reason not to do so. It is true that, if you want to come, it shows that God has been at work in you to draw you. But here is another truth: any sinner who *wants to come* is welcome. Do you want to come to God through Christ? Do not hold back then! Do not think of reasons why you must not! Come to Jesus, and do it *now*!

11: *Come to Me . . . For Ever!*

When Father says to Johnny, 'Come here!' he may only want Johnny for a moment. After that Johnny may return to his games. And that is what Johnny will do. He will run off with his friends to the fields or to the streets, while Father goes back to his chores. 'Come here' or 'Come to me' may mean no more than that.

But if this father is estranged from his son – what then? Then 'Come to me' may hide (or reveal) a longing to bring Johnny to his side for ever, to heal the old wounds, to re-create a 'closeness' between father and son. All of that, and much more, might be bound up in the phrase, 'Come to me'. The 'closeness' would not be mere physical closeness, of course. It would be that sympathy of feeling and enjoyment of one another that we call 'love'. Father would not seek it temporarily, either. He would want it to go on as long as they both should live.

Now all of this is a parable for us. It is a picture of the rupture between God and man that Jesus means to heal in saying, 'Come to Me'. 'Let us establish a *mutual* love,' He says, 'And let us do it for ever!'

All through this book I have been urging you to turn to Christ. I have told you that I am saying what Christ Himself has said. The words 'Come to Me' are His words. But there is a dimension about them of which, so far, I have said little or nothing. I am speaking of the idea contained in the words 'for ever'. Let me put two facts side by side, in order to make plain what I mean. Then I will talk about each in turn.

If you come to Christ, you *must* come to Him for ever.	If you come to Christ, you *will* come to Him for ever.

You will see at once that these two statements vary by only one word. Yet that one word is supremely important. Both statements are true, but they are quite different. One sentence speaks of your responsibility. You *must* come for ever. That is a huge demand. You dare not take it lightly. But once you have understood what that means, then there is this other thing that is also true. If you come to Christ, you *will* come for ever. In saying that I have left off speaking of your responsibility. I am speaking instead about the gracious power of God. Let us look at these two things, one at a time.

If you come to Christ, you *must* come for ever. That is what you are responsible to do. But what does that mean? It means two things. First of all, it tells you what your intention must be at the outset of your Christian life. Have you seen a sign that says, 'You've tried everything else, why not try Christ?' Well, that is *emphatically not* the spirit of Christianity! You are not to try Christ for a day or a week or a year as though He were some patent medicine to be cast aside if He does not quite do what you hoped He would do. That whole notion cannot be squared with the fact that Christ is Lord. You do not 'try' Him; you submit to Him! That is another thing entirely.

'You must come for ever', means one thing more. It means that you must go on with Christ in the midst of trial. You must stick it out. You must carry out your intention to serve Him for ever. You are not to be enticed by the allurements that Satan is certain to throw in your path. You must treat them as so many temptations to be resisted – to death, if necessary. 'No one', Jesus said, 'who puts his hand to the plow and looks back is fit for service in the kingdom of God' (*Luke 9:62*). You must never turn back!

All of this is just the kind of thing that marriage calls for. Marriage is a parable of the Christian life. God made it that way. I am speaking, of course, of marriage as God designed it. I know as well as you do the sort of mess that many among us have made of it. But the Lord told us what to do about marrying, and what He said is plain enough. It includes the command of Christ: 'What God has joined together, let man not separate' (*Mark 10:9*). In the wedding vows this is summed up with the words, 'Till death do us part!' That is as near to 'For ever!' as two people in this world can get.

Since it is no accident that these two things – our relationship to Christ and the relationship of husband and wife – are alike, let us compare them. First, God forbids trial marriages. You must intend to stay with the one you have chosen until death separates you. That is a chief point. And then, second, you must carry that intention out. It is to be done with love and affection, the kind of attitudes that lead to serving your life-mate.

I realise that many already have failed at both of these points in their marriages. Some of my readers may have been married more than once. That is not at all unusual in these days. If that is your case, you need the Savior, Jesus Christ! There is forgiveness with Him for all sin, including sins against husband or wife. But I am not speaking here of marriage, except as it pictures the Christian's relation to the Lord Jesus. There can be no trial union with Christ. You must settle that in your heart at the outset. And that is not all. From that time on, you are to serve Him with love and affection. You must not think of turning back! It is not faith, but doubt, that leads a man or woman to leave a back-door open, a way out. There can be no retreat for the child of God. That is what I mean when I say, 'If you come to Christ, you *must* come to Him for ever.'

Now here is the other side of the coin. This too is true: if you come to Christ you *will* come to Him for ever. You will not turn back. God will not allow you to do so. It is not simply that He will forbid it. No, in His grace and goodness He will gently draw you nearer and nearer to Himself and to His Son. You are not to enter the Christian life with confidence in your ability to hold out. That would be foolish. You have no power to do anything, much less to persevere in faith throughout life. You must *aim* to go on with Christ and never to give up following Him. But you must not suppose for an instant that you are powerful enough to manage it. Your confidence must be in Christ. Your hope of success must lie in God.

There is a great difference between our aim and our power to achieve our aim. It is like driving my automobile. When I climb into the front seat and start the engine I have a goal in mind. I want to get to Louisville or to Dayton. That is my aim. But that is not all I need. I must also have gasoline to take me there. If I were foolish enough to imagine that my good aim would take me to another city, I could sit there for ever and never make any progress. And so the Christian aims to follow Christ with all his heart. That is his goal. But the power to follow must come from Christ Himself. It must be the power of God. Will He give it? Indeed He will!

Let us hear Christ on this subject.

> All that the Father gives me will come to me, and whoever comes to me I will never drive away. For I have come down from heaven not to do my will but to do the will of him who sent me. And this is the will of him who sent me, that I shall lose none of all that he has given me, but raise them up at the last day. For my Father's will is that everyone who looks to the Son and believes in him

> shall have eternal life, and I will raise him up at the last day (*John 6:37–40*).

And let us add some words from the apostle Paul.

> Therefore, my dear friends . . . continue to work out your salvation with fear and trembling, for it is God who works in you to will and to act according to his good purpose (*Philippians 2:12–13*).

Taken together these verses encourage us in three ways. First, they show that Jesus is a determined Savior. He has made up His mind to bring all His people to Himself. He has set Himself to lose none, but to raise them all up and to give each of them eternal life. He will make no exceptions – not one!

Secondly, Paul's words point up the path that Jesus means to take us along. It is a way of willing and acting according to God's will. Here, however, is the thing to note. The Christian is not left to himself. Certainly he must 'work out' his salvation. He must push on in godliness and righteousness. But there is something that lies behind his efforts. 'It is God,' Paul says, 'who works in you!' And what is it that He does? 'God . . . works in you to will and to act according to his good purpose.' What more could a believer ask? Here is our hope of holding out, of going on. We do not trust ourselves. We have no power. Power belongs to God, not to ourselves. We look to God!

Finally, there is a third thing in these verses to cheer us and to draw us on. It is hinted at in the phrases, 'All that the Father gives me,' and 'all that he has given me.' Here Jesus offers us a glimpse into His own relation to His Father. Behind these words stands an enormous truth that explains, in part, the sure grip with which God holds believers. That truth is this: God loves His Son and has promised Christ a people for Himself that no man can number. God means to keep that promise, though all hell oppose it.

One New Testament writer tells us that Jesus went to the cross with a great future joy in sight. Here are his words:

> Let us fix our eyes on Jesus, the author and perfecter of our faith, who *for the joy set before him* endured the cross, scorning its shame, and sat down at the right hand of the throne of God (*Hebrews 12:2*).

What was that joy? No doubt it was His exaltation. His sitting down to rule at the right hand of His Father. But that is not all: there is more. Jesus' joy will not be complete until He has all around Him the men and women and children that He redeemed at the cross. Listen to this. Jesus is speaking:

> Father, I want those you have given to me to be with me where I am, and to see my glory, the glory you have given me because you loved me before the creation of the world (*John 17:24*).

Do you suppose that the Father will refuse Jesus this request? No, He will not! He will not turn a deaf ear to Jesus' prayer because that moment is the goal toward which all human history has been moving. From the instant Adam rebelled, God has been working to restore men and women to Himself. He has looked forward to the day when Christ will be Lord of all, when Jesus will have all His children around Him admiring His glory, and when all those who have defied His lordship are cast away for ever. God has been steering toward that hour. He has not hurried. Quite often no human eye could have traced His path. But that did not matter. It does not matter now. What is important is the certainty that God will reach His goal. That is as sure as God Himself.

Will you be one of the company who admire Christ in that day? If so, you must come to Him now. Trust in Jesus Christ! Do you have sins to be forgiven? Who can forgive them but the Son of God? Do you lack power over your sin? Where will you get it but at His feet? 'Come to me,' Jesus said, and He meant it. Do you need Christ as Savior and Lord and Sustainer, and do you feel that need? Then come! Come just as you are. 'All that the Father gives me will come to me,' said Jesus. That shows God's side of the work. But what if you come halting and trembling and fearful that you will not be welcome? What, then? Well, here is the promise for you: 'and whoever comes to me I will never drive away!' Those, too, are Jesus' words. Come to Him, and make them your very own!

Come, ye sinners, poor and needy,
Weak and wounded, sick and sore;
Jesus ready stands to save you,
Full of pity, joined with power:
He is able, He is able,
He is willing: doubt no more.

Come, ye weary, heavy-laden,
Bruised and mangled by the fall;
If you tarry till you're better,
You will never come at all;
Not the righteous, not the righteous –
Sinners Jesus came to call.

Let not conscience make you linger,
Nor of fitness fondly dream;
All the fitness He requireth
Is to feel your need of Him:
This He gives you, this He gives you;
'Tis the Spirit's rising beam.

(Joseph Hart, 1712–1768)

12: *A Closing Word*

In these pages I have pled with you to turn to Christ. Very likely we have never met. Yet I wanted to do for your soul what others – some of them strangers to me – have done for mine. I could not do more; I would not do less. My prayer as I write this is: 'Open my reader's mind, Lord, whoever he or she may be, to see the attractiveness of Jesus Christ!' May God grant my request!

And if you come to Christ, what then? Well, then you are His slave as well as His beloved. And that requires that you henceforth serve Him with joy and gratitude – for ever. Nothing less will do *as a goal*, though you may often stumble.

But where will you find His will for you? If you are to serve Him, what are you to do?

There is a simple answer to this question, but it is not an easy answer. It will demand your attention for the rest of your life. The answer is this: the Bible contains God's will for you. You must learn it; you must know what it says. And you must do it.

But how will you learn it? You will read it, of course. Let me suggest that you start by reading and thinking about the Gospel of John, the fourth book in the New Testament. That will get you under way. Read it through, from beginning to end, and do it more than once. Perhaps five or ten times would be a good start. And ask the Lord to help you understand and act on what you read.

But there is something else you must do. You must fix it in your mind that you are not to learn the Scriptures by yourself. The Bible was meant to be understood in the gathering of believers. There each has the opportunity and responsibility to correct and encourage others in their understanding. It is a great favor from God that we may own Bibles. But it is clear that that was not possible when the Scriptures were penned. The invention of printing has allowed us to have copies of God's Word. Throughout the greater part of church history, however, that was impossible for all but the very rich.

God, in His wisdom, has provided us with teachers to help us. We must not despise His provision. Rather, we must hear what they say in the congregation, week by week. The writer of *Hebrews* put it this way:

> Let us not give up meeting together, as some are in the habit of doing, but let us encourage one another – and all the more as you see the Day approaching (*Hebrews 10:25*).

The prospect of the end, when God will renew the universe, is to stir us up. We must not fold our hands if we are servants of Christ. We must be faithful to Him and we must work and pray and study together. He has called us together to be His 'body'. We, in turn, must draw closer to other believers. We must learn from them the ways of Christ. We must listen attentively to them when they explain to us the Word of God.

Also, let me guard against one particular misunderstanding. As you may know, there was a great struggle in the sixteenth century to give the Scriptures to the common man. In that battle the cry was raised for 'private interpretation' of God's Word. It is the right of every man, it was said, to interpret the Bible for himself. No Pope, nor priest, nor preacher has authority over the conscience.

After all, some said, the Scriptures are clear. Each man must decide for himself the meaning of the Scriptures. And he must act accordingly!

In my judgment that battle was necessary and right. May God preserve us from falling back into the old way! We dare not allow others to know the Bible on our behalf and rest on their knowledge to take us to heaven. That would be a return to darkness!

But I must add two cautions to what I have said. The first is this. The Bible is our standard by which we are to test the teaching of others. It was never intended to replace their teaching. It was given to us to sift out the truth from the error in what we hear. I may illustrate this by an experience the Apostle Paul and others had when preaching in the Greek city Berea. They had been driven out of Thessalonica by those who rejected Paul's message. Berea was the next stop on their tour. Keep in mind that Paul speaks with Christ's authority, as Christ's special envoy.

> On arriving [in Berea], they went to the Jewish synagogue. Now the Bereans were of more noble character than the Thessalonians, for they received the message with great eagerness and examined the Scriptures every day to see if what Paul said was true. Many of the Jews believed, as did also a number of prominent Greek women and many Greek men (*Acts 17:10–12*).

These Bereans are our models. They listened eagerly; so must we! But that was not all they did. They 'examined the Scriptures'. They checked up on Paul, to see whether what he said was in keeping with God's Word. We must do that as well.

My other caution is this. We must not misunderstand the 'clarity' of Scripture about which the sixteenth-century Reformers spoke. These men were fighting for the basic elements of the gospel story. They contended that the Bible was 'clear' on how a man may become right with God. And on that score they were surely correct. Every man is right with God if he trusts wholeheartedly in Jesus Christ. And no person is right with God in any other way.

But this does not mean that Scripture has no depths that are difficult to fathom. Not at all! The keenest intellect cannot find out all that God has revealed. There is always more, and more again. Yet faithful men have gone before us, exploring God's truth. We are fools if we do not seek to follow them. Only we must not follow them blindly. We must have the 'Berean' spirit. We must compare their teaching with the Word of God.

How can you find a group of Christians with which to worship and study? I wish I could say simply, 'Any church or chapel will do.' But I am afraid that statement is much too broad. As with other organisations, there are churches and there are churches. Some sincerely seek to know God's Word; others, unhappily, are merely social clubs with Christ largely in the background. Somehow you will have to tell one from the other.

Here are my suggestions. First, if someone has given you this book as a gift you may turn to him or her for help. Ask to go with that person to the congregation where they meet with other Christians. It is likely that you will find a warm welcome. Then judge for yourself whether the group is seriously interested in knowing the Word of God. Do not fall into the trap of judging other things on that first visit. That is the key – an earnest desire to know and do God's Word.

But perhaps you purchased this book or received it from a stranger. In that case I suggest that you write to the publishers of this book for help. In most cases they will be able to direct you to a Christian not too far away.

And that, in turn, should lead you to a church or chapel where you may apply the test I have described above.

This is my last chance to speak to you in this book. What shall I say? Some months ago I came across the following plea. It was written by John Mason, a seventeenth-century preacher. It is my next-to-last word to you.

> Have you sins, or have you none? If you have, whither should you go, but to the Lamb of God, which taketh away the sins of the world? . . . Come as you are; come poor, come needy, come naked, come empty, come wretched, only come, only believe; His heart is free, His arms are open; 'tis His joy and His crown to receive you. If you are willing, He never was otherwise.

My last word is the word of Jesus Christ Himself:

> Come to me, all you who are weary and burdened, and I will give you rest. Take my yoke upon you and learn from me, for I am gentle and humble in heart, and you will find rest for your souls. For my yoke is easy and my burden is light (*Matthew 11:27–29*).